Venn Perplexors

Level B

MindWare®
brainy toys for kids of all ages®

www.MINDWAREonline.com

A MindWare® Original!

Our entire selection of Brainy Toys for Kids of All Ages® is available at www.MINDWAREonline.com, or by calling us at 800-999-0398 to request a catalog.

Coloring Books

Each of our coloring books offer one of a kind patterns, textures and styles you make your own by choosing how to bring them to life.

Animal Habitats Series
Creature Camouflage Series
Designs Series
Lights Series
Modern Patterns Series
Mosaics Series
Quilts Series
Scapes Series
Transformations Series

Puzzle Books

Our puzzle books build skills in many areas—from logic to math, spatial reasoning to verbal skills.

Addition Adventures
Analogy Challenges
Clip Clue Puzzles
Code Breakers
Decimal Destinations
Deducibles
Directive Detective
Division Designs
Fast Fact Trivia
Fraction Finders
Grid Perplexors
Logic Links
Math Path Puzzles
Math Perplexors
More Multiplication Mosaics
Multiplication Mosaics
Noodlers
Number Circuits
Number Junctions
Perplexors
Sequencers
Subtraction Secrets
Tactic Twisters
Tan-Tastic Tangrams
Venn Perplexors
Word Winks
Word Wise

Games and Activities

Building blocks to strategic games, mystery puzzles to imaginative play — enhance abstract thinking and reasoning skills with our ingenious games and activities.

Bella's Mystery Decks
Blik-Blok
Block Buddies
Chaos
Cross-Eyed
Flip 4
Gambit
Hue Knew?
Logic Links Game
Make Your Own Mask Kit
Noodlers Game
Pattern Play
Qwirkle
Tally Rally

Squzzles

Configure nine 3 x 3 pieces into a square where all images match up on every single side. Three challenging puzzles per box.

3-D Scramblers
Animal Babies
Botanicals
Creature Kingdom
Creepy Crawlers
Dinosaurs!
Illusions
Insect Infested
Nocturnal Animals
Optical Illusions
Play Ball!
Wings & Wheels
World Money

1/2008

A word about the author:
Evelyn has undergraduate and master degrees in mathematics, specialist and doctoral degrees in mathematics education, and both regular and Montessori certification. She has taught elementary, middle school, high school, college, and graduate school levels. She is currently teaching kindergarten because that's her favorite age. As a parent of three, she has had much experience providing children with stimulating educational activities, not only in the classroom, but also in the home. She is the author of several puzzle books, in addition to the Venn Perplexors series.

"This book is dedicated to two of my most wonderful encouragers, my husband Ralph and my sister Betty, and to the Creator God who shares with us the gift of creativity."
Evelyn B. Christensen

Design by Kristine Mudd

EAN 978-1-892069-47-4
SKU 17002

MindWare® brainy toys for kids of all ages®

for other MindWare products visit our website
www.MINDWAREonline.com

Overview of Venn Diagrams

Venn diagrams, first used by English mathematician John Venn (1834-1923), are a method of using rectangles and circles (or ovals) to show relationships between sets. In a Venn diagram, each circle represents a specific set. If something belongs to a set, it is inside the circle designated for that set. If everything in a set belongs to a larger set, then we say that the first set is a subset of the second.

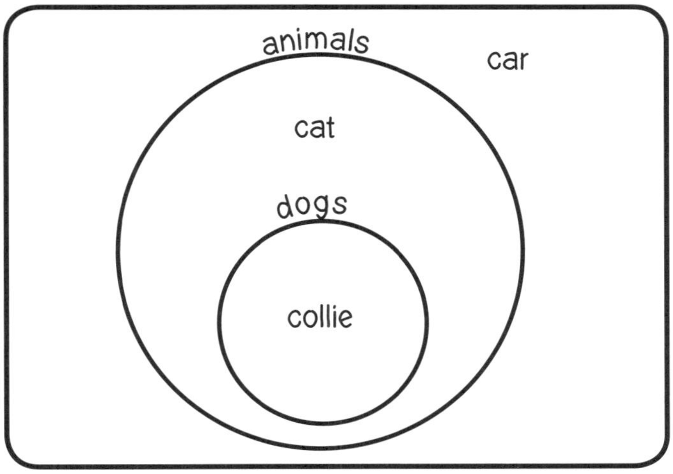

Here's an example:

The circle for the dogs set is drawn completely inside the circle for the animals set, making it clear that dogs are a subset of animals.

Anything that does not belong to a set, such as car, is placed outside the set's circle.

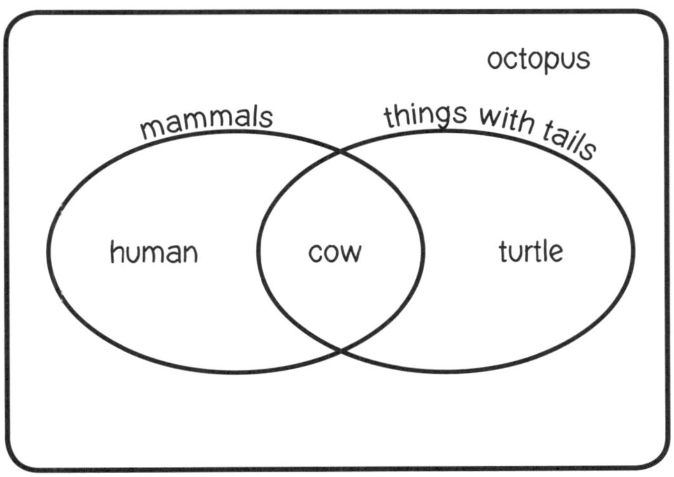

If two sets have things that belong to both sets, then we show this in a Venn diagram by having the two circles (or ovals) overlap. The section that belongs to both circles is called the "intersection."

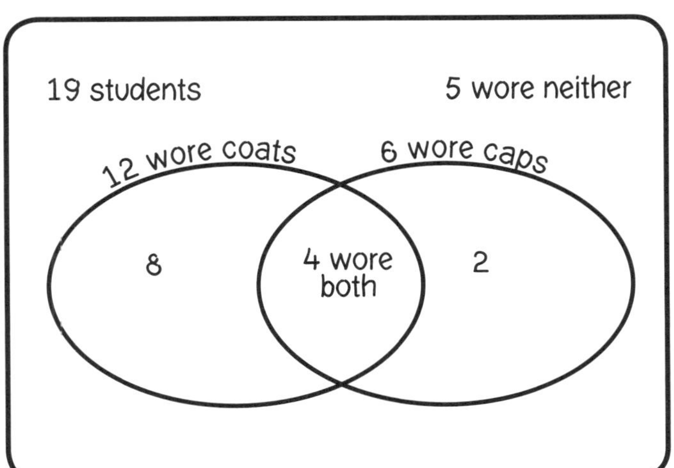

Sometimes we are interested in the number of elements that are in each set, or subset, rather than the names of the elements.

This Venn diagram represents 19 students on their way to school. From it we know:

- 4 students wore a coat and a cap
- 8 wore a coat but not a cap
- 5 did not wear a coat or a cap
- 2 wore a cap but not a coat
- 12 wore a coat
- 6 wore a cap

How to solve the puzzles:

Example 1:

The 6th grade class took a poll on what kinds of pizza students like to eat, and here are the results: 7 students like pepperoni pizza, 13 like mushroom, 5 like both mushroom and pepperoni pizza, and 4 students like neither. How many students are in the class?

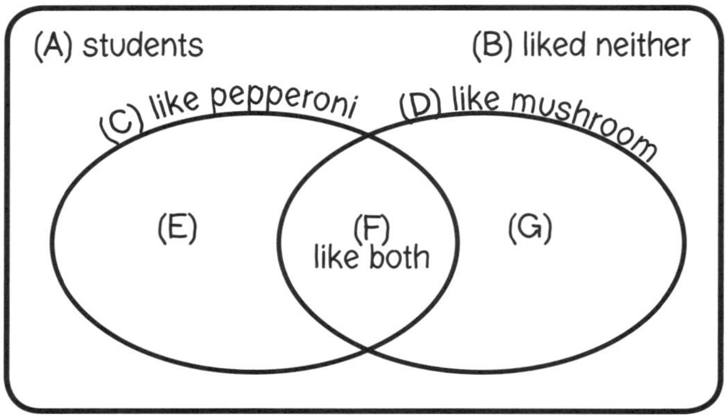

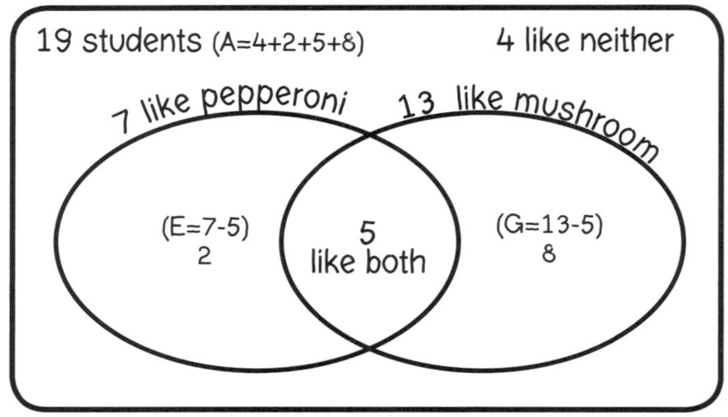

Step-by-step solution:

Write: The story gives you information for B, C, D, and F, so fill in those values first (shown above left).

Solve: C = the sum of E and F, so E = C – F
D = the sum of F and G, so G = D – F
A, the answer to the question, is found by adding the four sets: A = B + E + F + G

Record: 19 students are in the class.

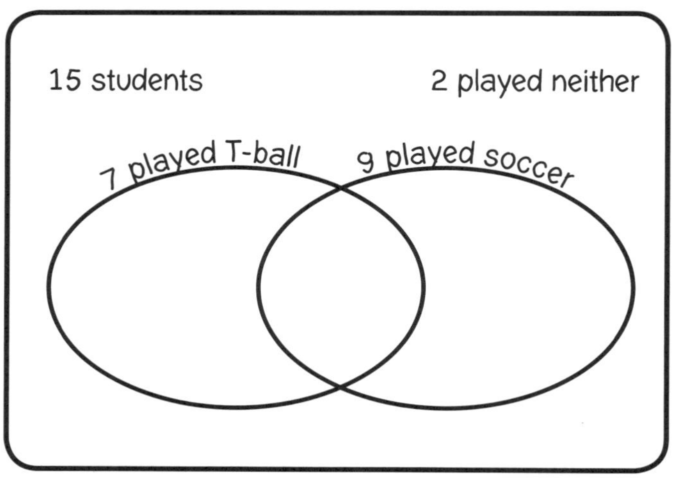

Example 2:

15 students were discussing sports. They discovered that 7 of them had played T-ball, 9 of them had played soccer, and only 2 of them had played neither. How many had played both soccer and T-ball.

Step-by-step solution:

Write: The story gives you information for A, B, C, and D, so fill in those values first.

Solve: A = B + C + G and 15 = 2 + 7 + G, so G = 6
D = F + G and 9 = F + 6, so F = 3
C = E + F and 7 = E + 3, so E = 4

Record: 3 students had played both soccer and T-ball.

Venn Perplexors

The Rhyme

There was an old woman
who lived in a shoe.
She had so many children,
She didn't know what to do.

So she gave them some broth
with lots of bread,
And kissed them all soundly
and sent them to bed.

The Clues

The old woman in the shoe had 14 children who liked bread and 9 who liked broth.

Of those, 4 liked both.

3 of her children liked neither.

Puzzle #1

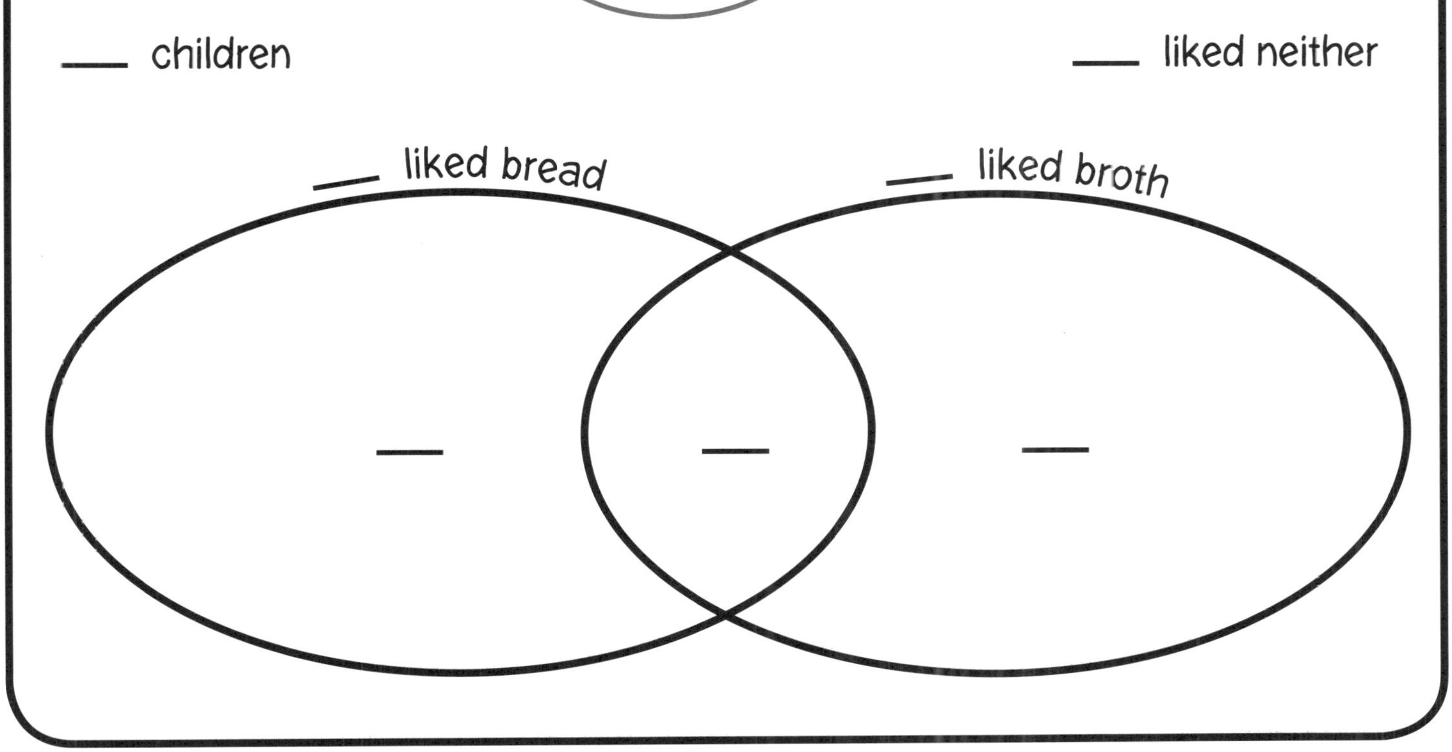

How many children did the old woman have? ______

Venn Perplexors

The Rhyme

Sing a song of sixpence,
A pocket full of rye;
Four and twenty blackbirds
Baked in a pie.

When the pie was opened,
The birds began to sing:
Wasn't that a dainty dish
To set before the king?

The Clues

24 birds were baked in the pie.

When the pie was opened 18 birds began to sing.

11 of those flew away singing.

Only 1 didn't fly or sing.

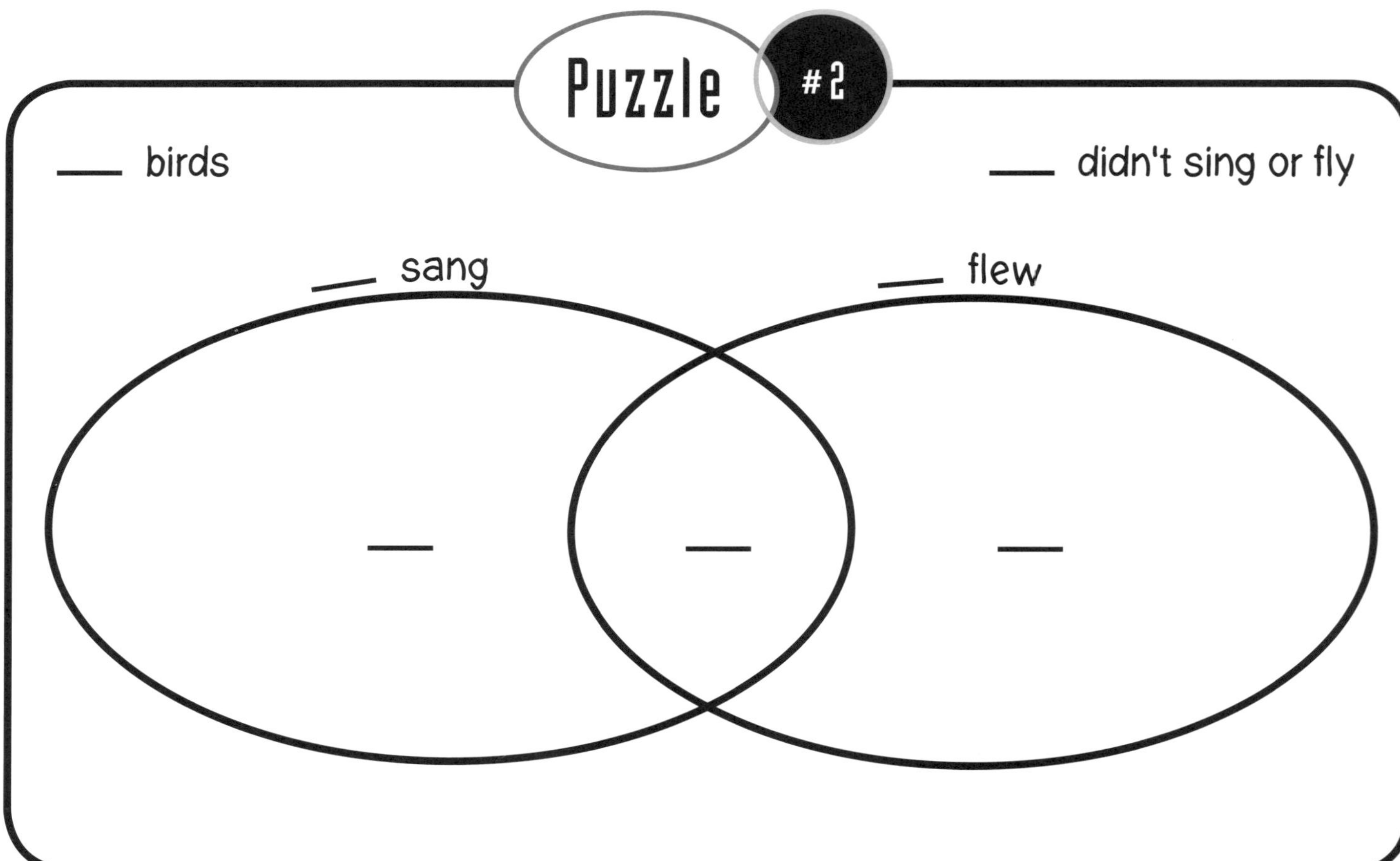

How many blackbirds flew away? ______

Venn Perplexors

The Rhyme

Little Bo-Peep has lost her sheep
And doesn't know where to find them;
Leave them alone, and they'll come home,
Wagging their tails behind them.

The Clues

Little Bo-Peep has a flock of 27 sheep.

15 sheep are not lost, but the rest are.

3 of the lost sheep are lambs.

Puzzle #3

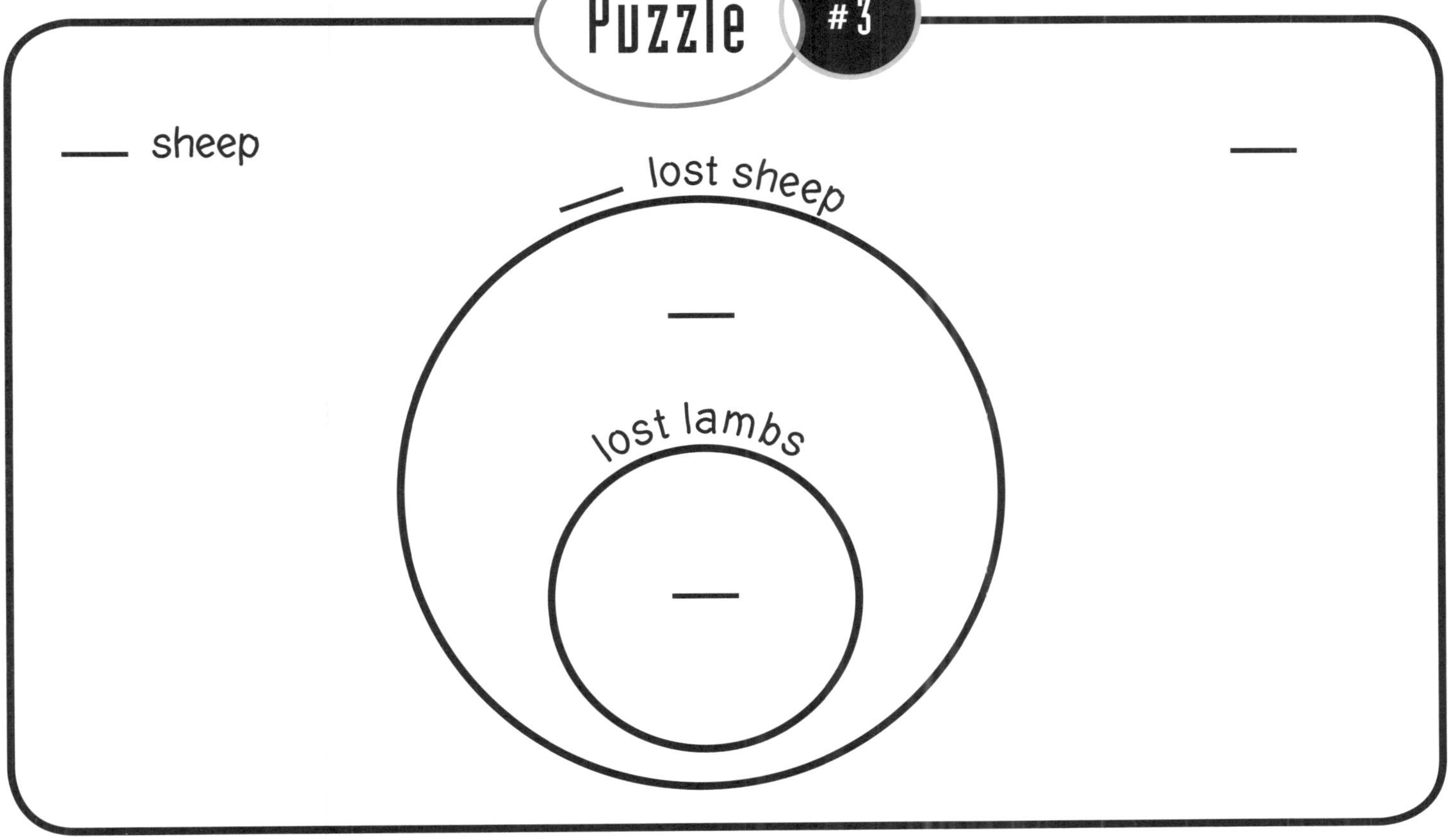

How many of the lost sheep are rams or ewes? ______

Venn Perplexors

The Rhyme

Cobbler, cobbler, mend my shoe,
Get it done by half past two;
Stitch it up, and stitch it down,
Make the finest shoes in town.

The Clues

The poor cobbler has 13 pairs of shoes to work on today.

By half past two, he's worked on the tops of 5 pairs.

On 3 of those he's done the bottoms also.

He's worked on the bottoms of a total of 6 pairs.

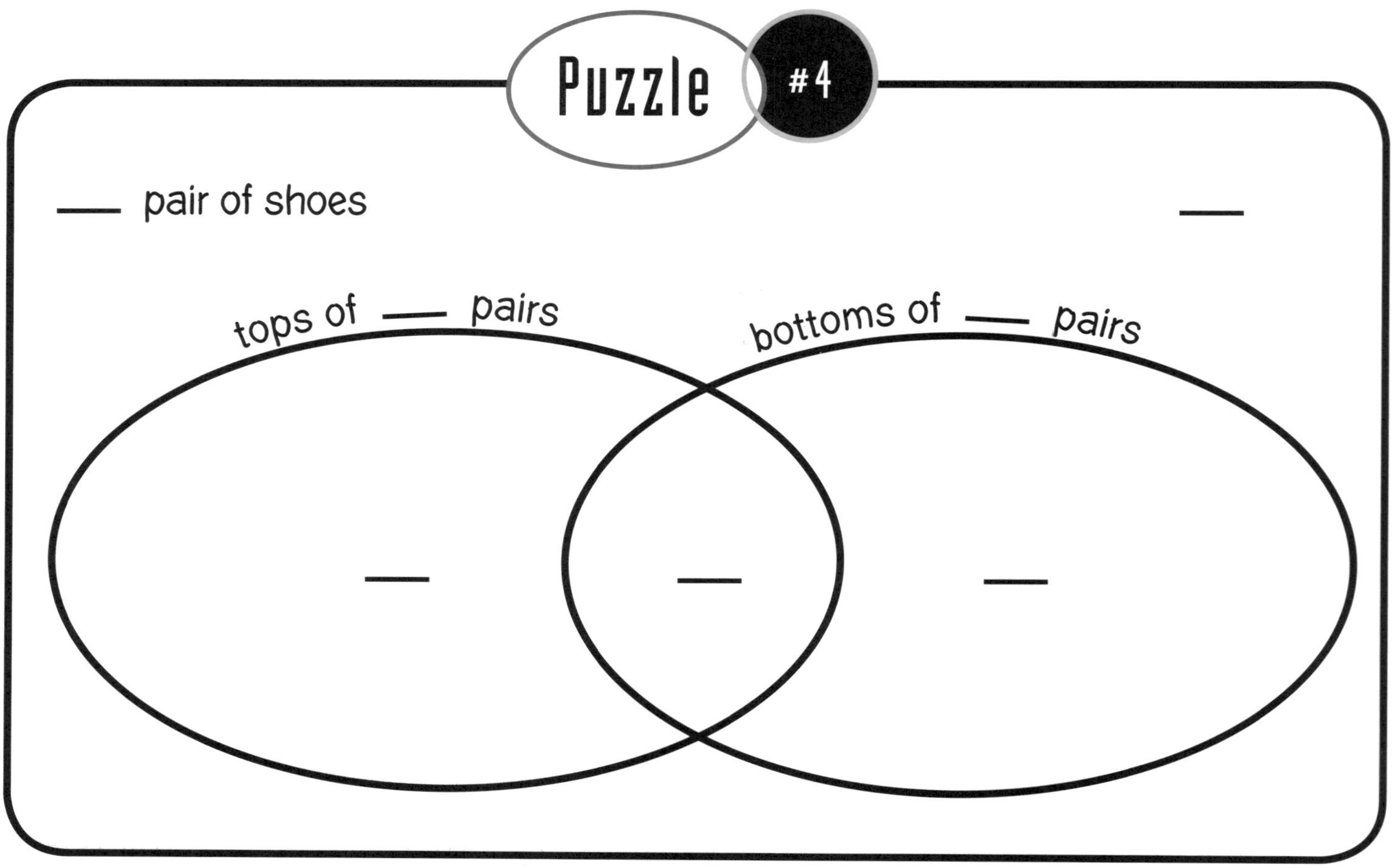

How many pairs has he not worked on at all? ______

Venn Perplexors

The Rhyme

One, two, buckle my shoe.
Three, four, shut the door.
Five, six, pick up sticks.
Seven, eight, lay them straight.

The Clues

You have 6 sticks you picked up and 8 more sticks you laid down.

5 of the sticks are green.

4 of the sticks are crooked.

7 of the sticks are not crooked or green.

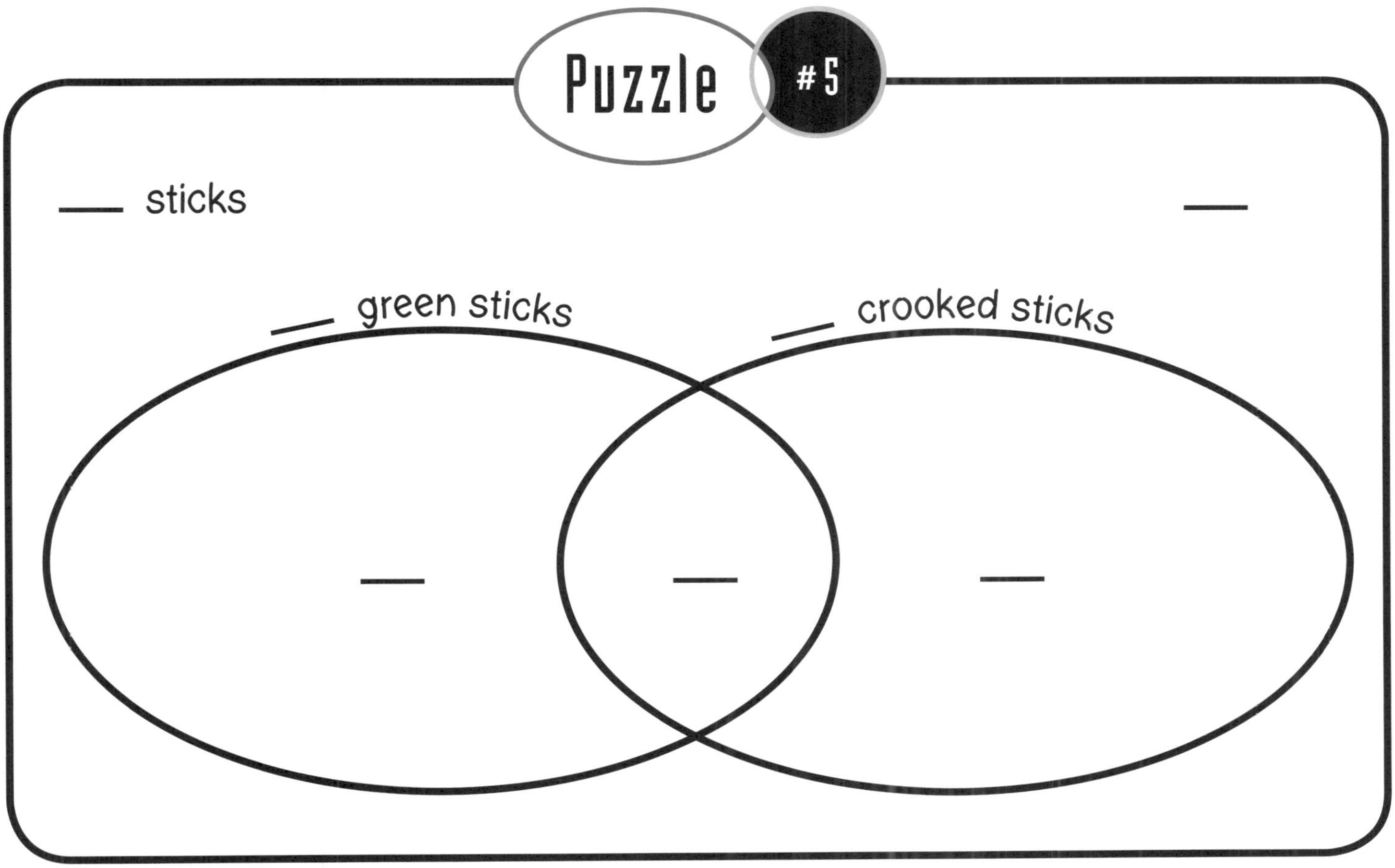

How many crooked, green sticks do you have? ______

Venn Perplexors

The Rhyme

I saw a ship a-sailing,
A-sailing on the sea;
And, oh! it was all laden
With pretty things for thee!

The four and twenty sailors,
That stood upon the decks
Were four and twenty white mice,
With scarves about their necks.

The Clues

16 of the 24 sailors on the ship were hard at work swabbing the decks.

18 of the sailors were singing.

4 of the sailors were neither singing nor swabbing.

Puzzle #6

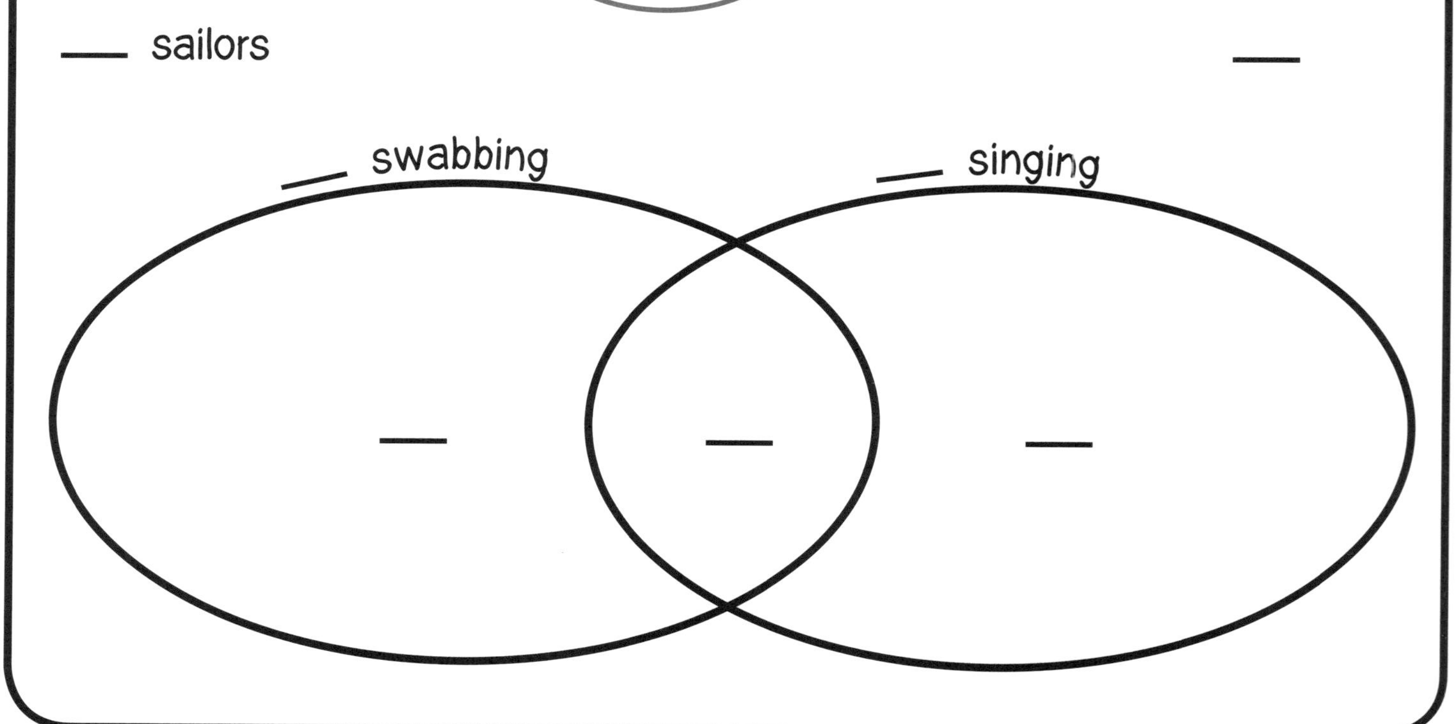

How many were swabbing, but not singing? ______

Venn Perplexors

The Rhyme

One potato, two potatoes,
Three potatoes, four,
Five potatoes, six potatoes,
Seven potatoes, more!

The Clues

A group of children were discussing how they liked potatoes.

They discovered that 16 of them liked mashed potatoes, 20 of them liked French fries, 14 of them liked mashed potatoes and French fries, and 1 person didn't like mashed potatoes or French fries.

Puzzle #7

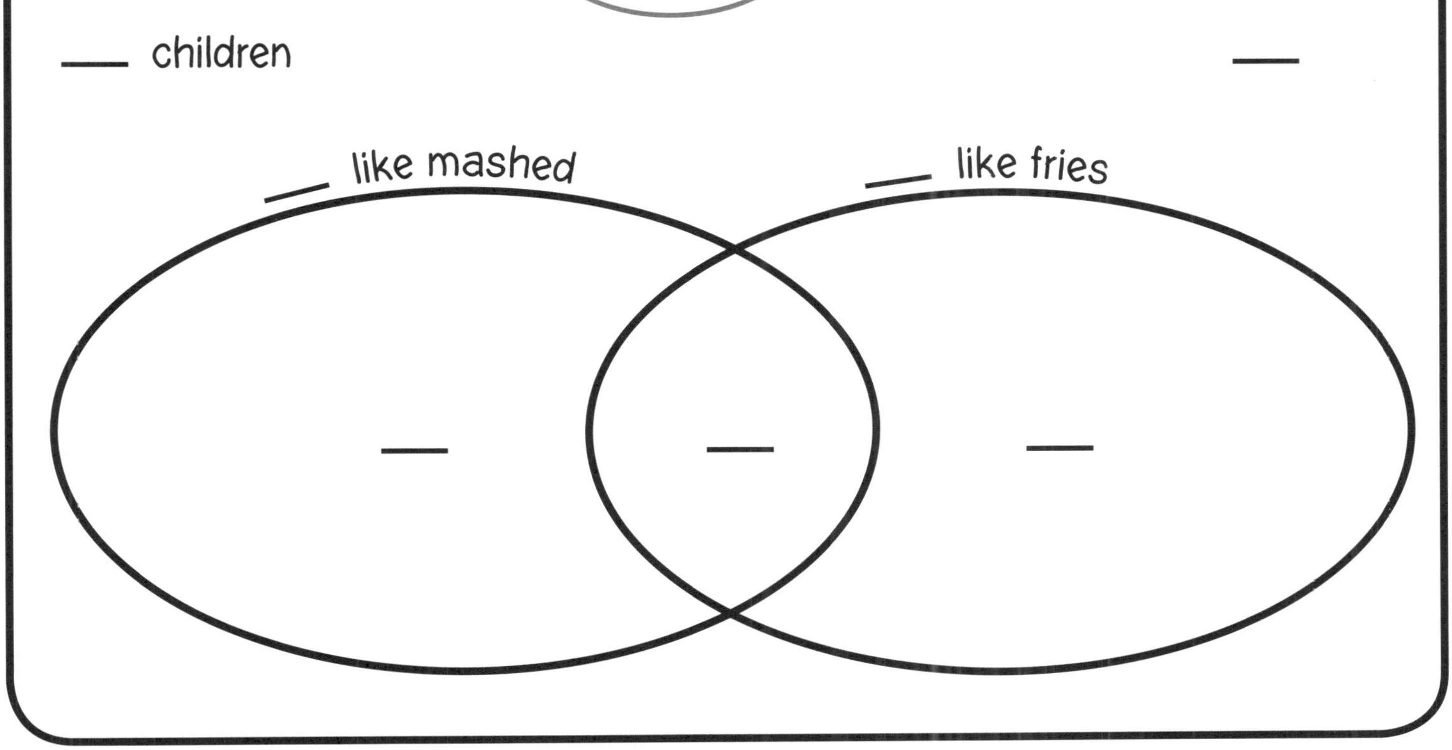

How many children were in the group? ______

Venn Perplexors

The Rhyme

Simple Simon met a pieman
Going to the fair.
Said Simple Simon to the pieman,
"Let me taste your ware."
Said the pieman to Simple Simon,
"Show me first your penny."
Said Simple Simon to the pieman,
"Indeed, I have not any."

The Clues

The pieman had four kinds of pies to sell: cherry, strawberry, rhubarb, and strawberry rhubarb.

Of his 18 pies 7 had strawberries, 9 had rhubarb, and 5 had cherries.

Puzzle #8

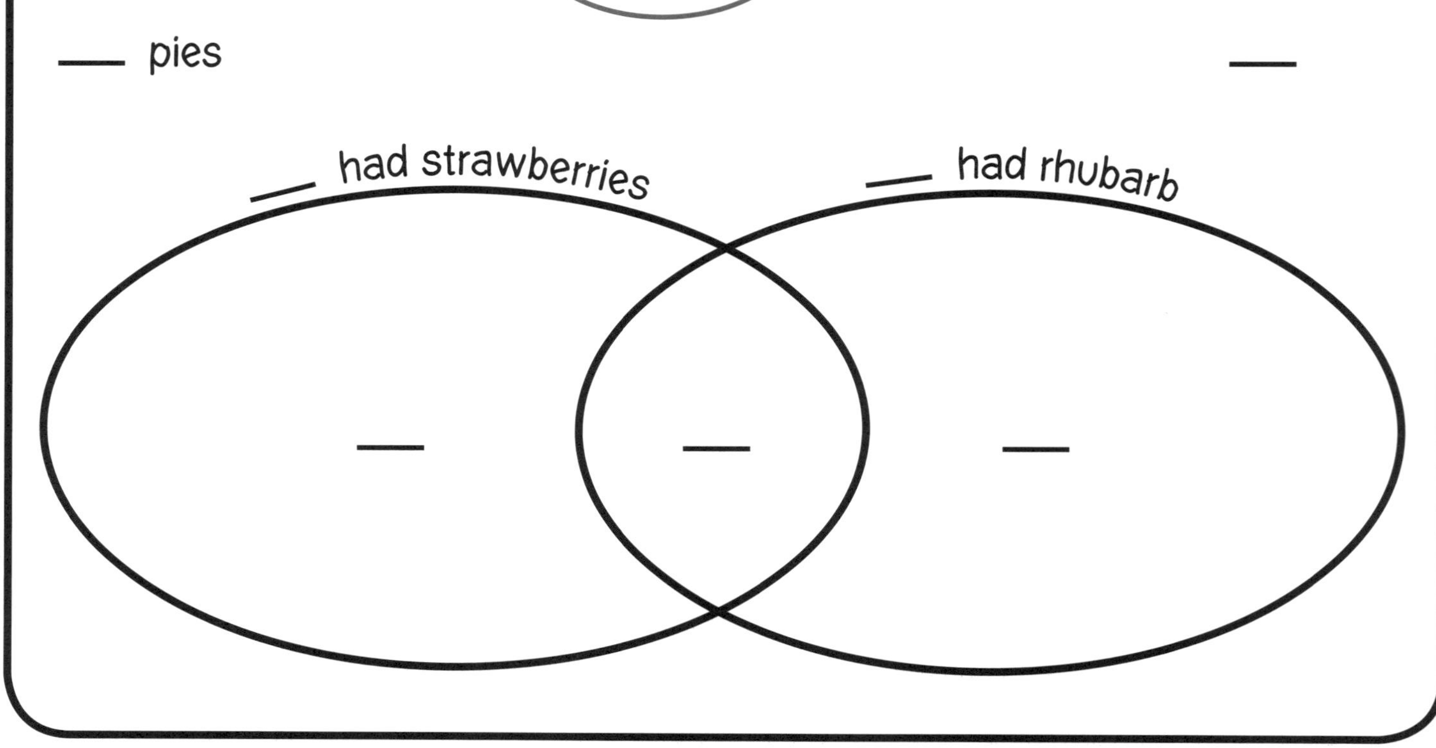

How many had both strawberries and rhubarb? ______

Venn Perplexors

The Rhyme

Hark, hark, the dogs do bark,
Beggars are coming to town;
Some in rags and some in tags,
And some in velvet gown.

The Clues

11 beggars are coming to town.

2 of them are in velvet gowns.

8 are in rags.

7 are in tags*.

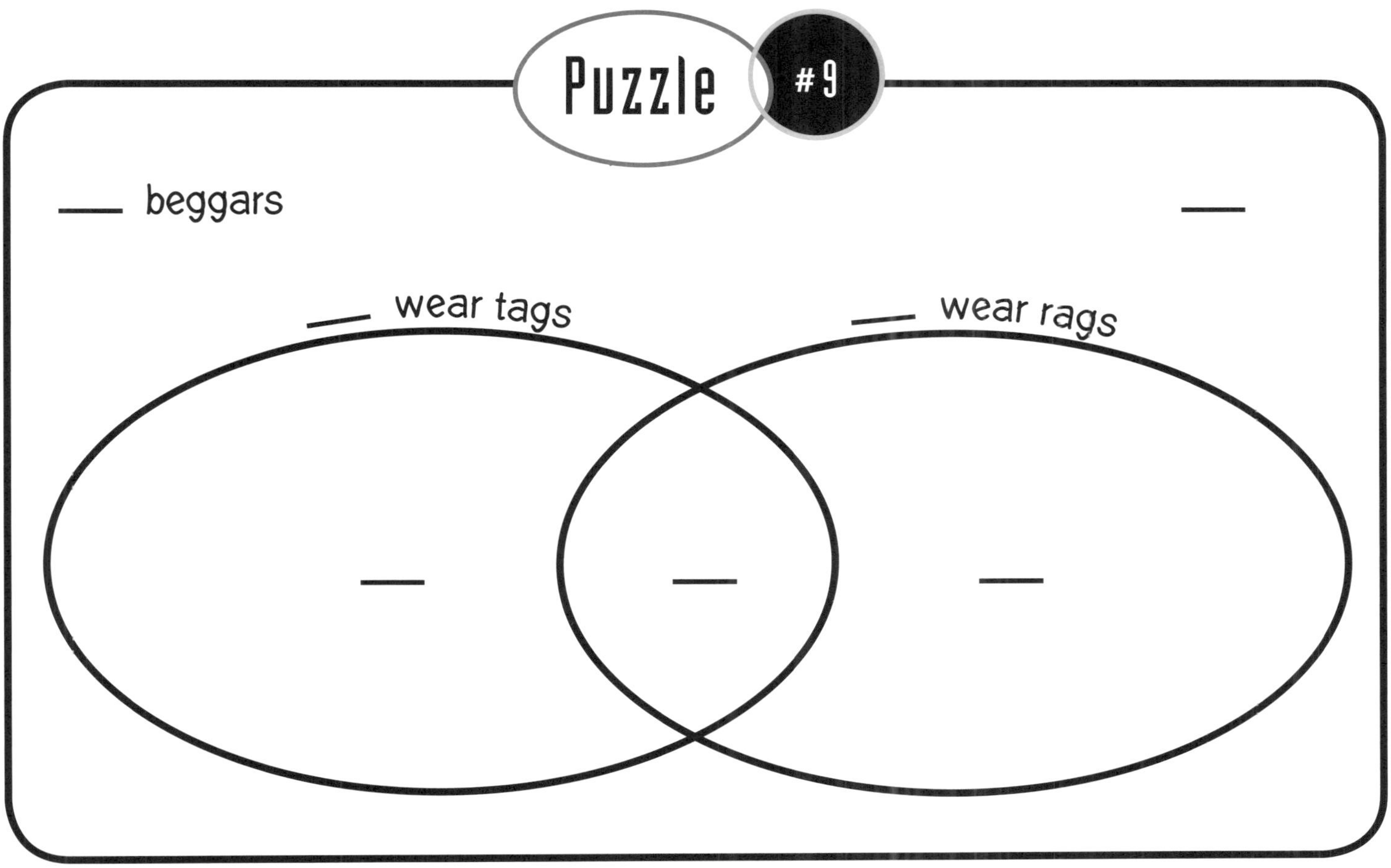

How many beggars are in rags and tags? ______

Note: "tags" originally meant a hanging end like a torn shirttail.

Venn Perplexors

The Rhyme

Little Boy Blue, come blow your horn,
The sheep's in the meadow,
the cow's in the corn.

Where is the little boy
who looks after the sheep?
He's under the haystack fast asleep.

The Clues

13 of the animals Little Boy Blue tends have gotten into the corn.

11 have gotten into the meadow.

5 have actually gotten into both!

Only 4 of his animals stayed where they belong.

Puzzle #10

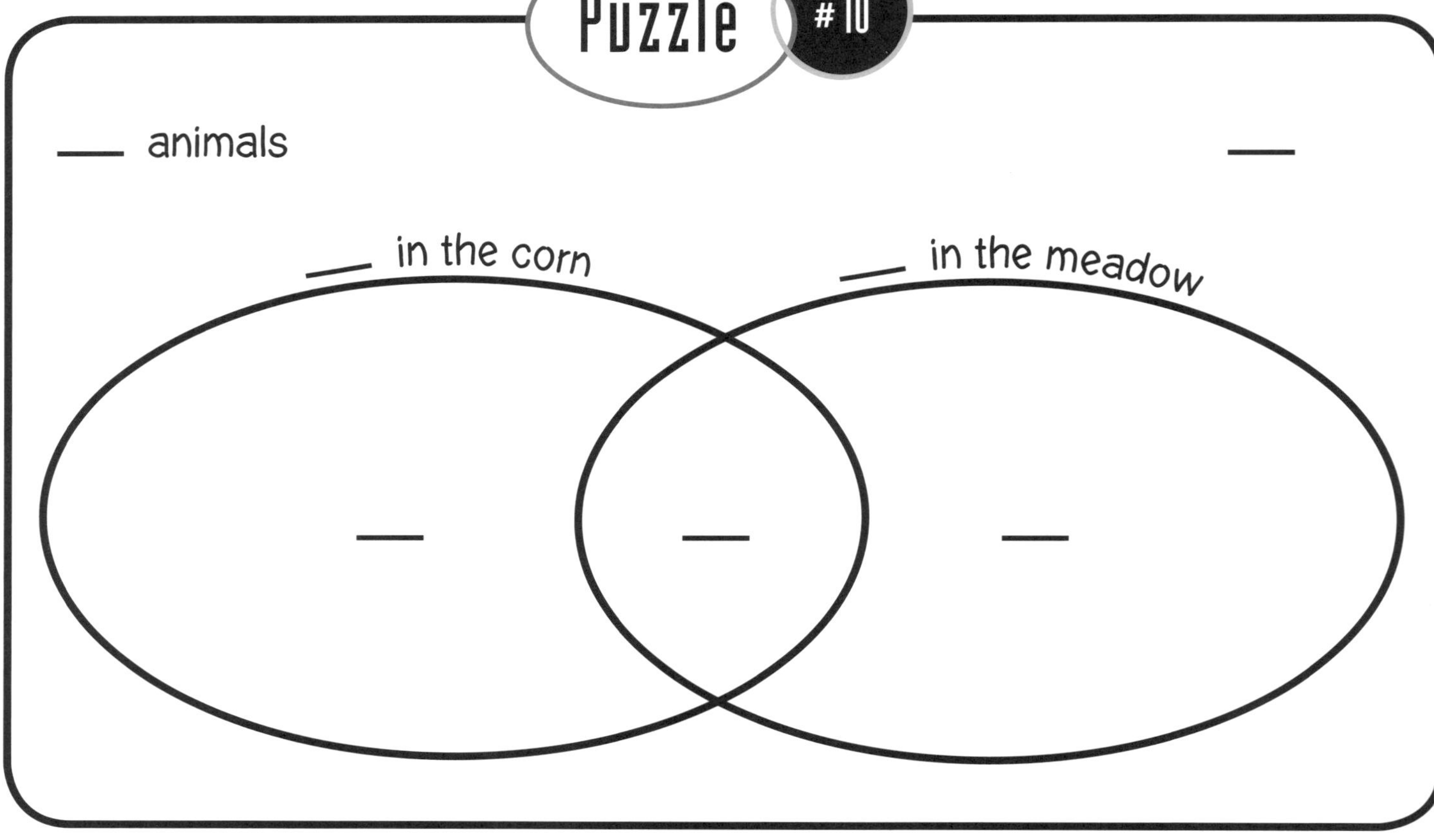

How many animals does Little Boy Blue tend? ______

Venn Perplexors

The Rhyme

London Bridge is falling down,
Falling down, falling down.
London Bridge is falling down,
My fair lady.

Build it up with wood and clay,
Wood and clay, wood and clay.
Build it up with wood and clay,
My fair lady.

The Clues

The workers are bringing wood and clay to build up London Bridge.

All of them are bringing one or the other or both. 10 are bringing wood. 14 are bringing clay.

Of those, 7 are bringing both wood and clay.

Puzzle #11

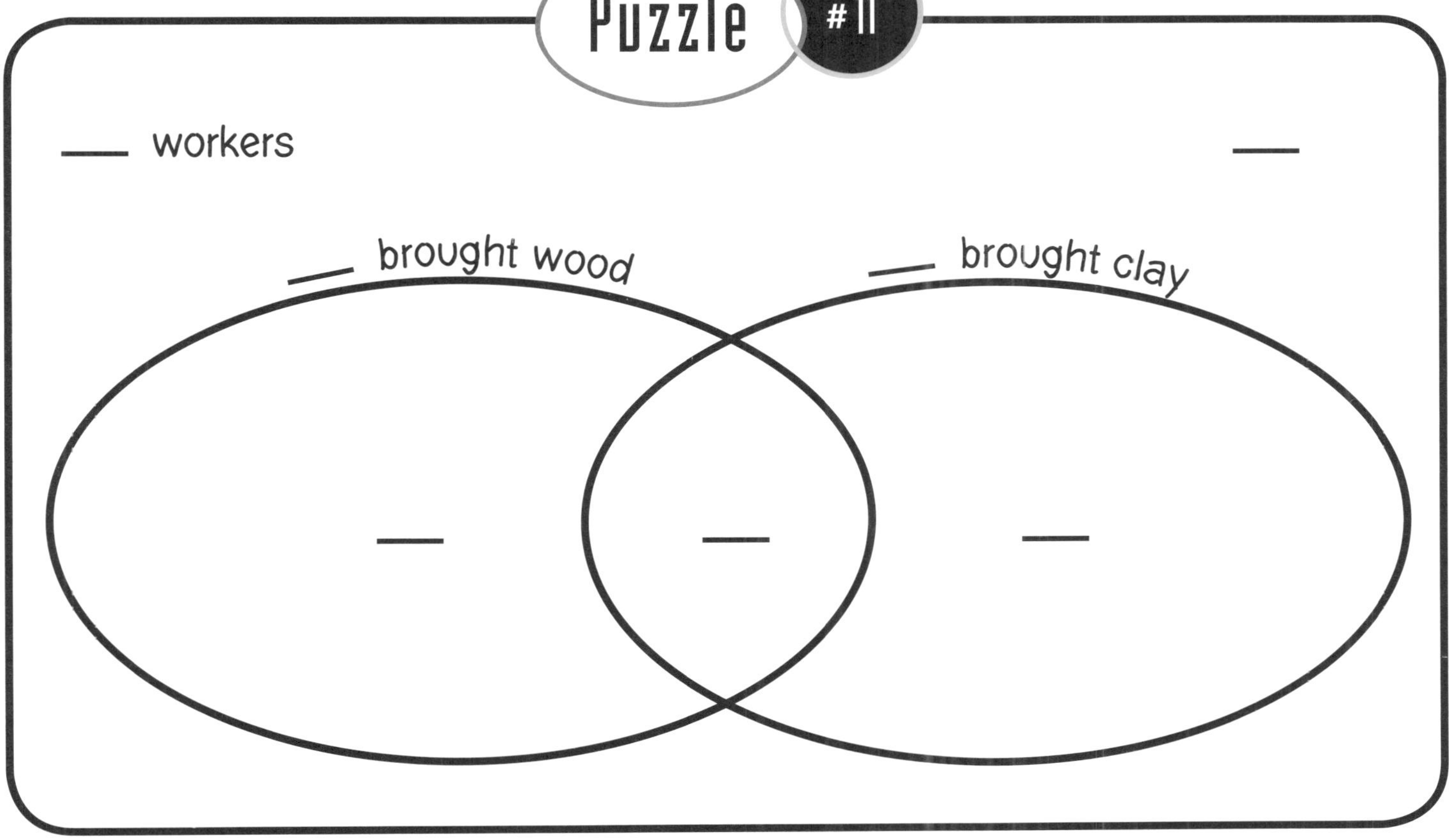

How many workers are there? ______

Venn Perplexors

The Rhyme

Smiling girls, rosy boys,
Come and buy my little toys:
Monkeys made of gingerbread,
And sugar horses painted red.

The Clues

The children love gingerbread monkeys and sugar horses.

9 children each buy a monkey and 11 children each buy a sugar horse.

2 children can't buy because they didn't bring their money.

There are 15 children in all.

Puzzle #12

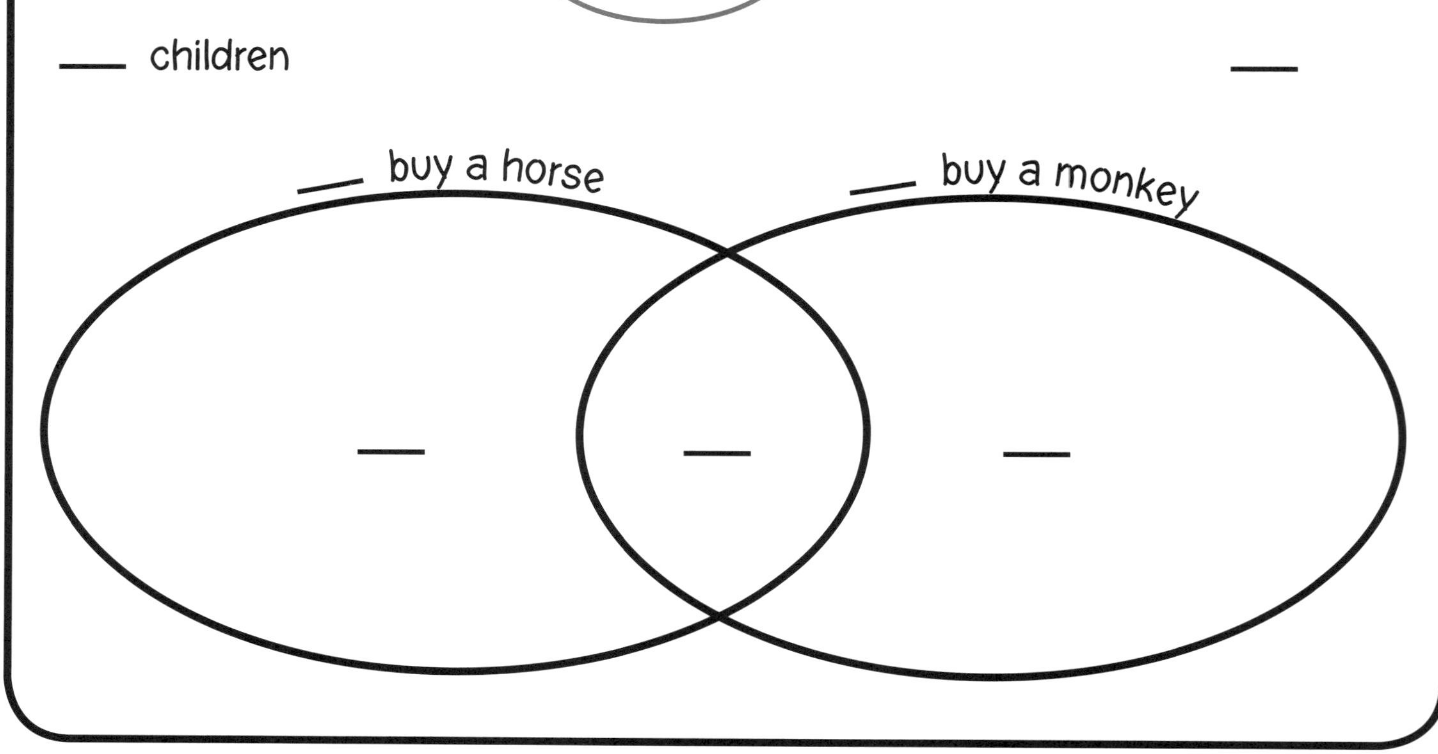

How many children bought both a monkey and a horse? ______

Venn Perplexors

The Rhyme

The Queen of Hearts
She made some tarts,
All on a summer's day.

The Knave of Hearts
He stole those tarts,
And took them clean away.

The Clues

The Queen of Hearts made 3 trays of tarts, with 12 on each tray.

Fortunately, the Knave of Hearts didn't see one of the trays and only stole those he saw.

As soon as he got to a hiding place, he ate 1/3 of the tarts he'd stolen.

Puzzle #13

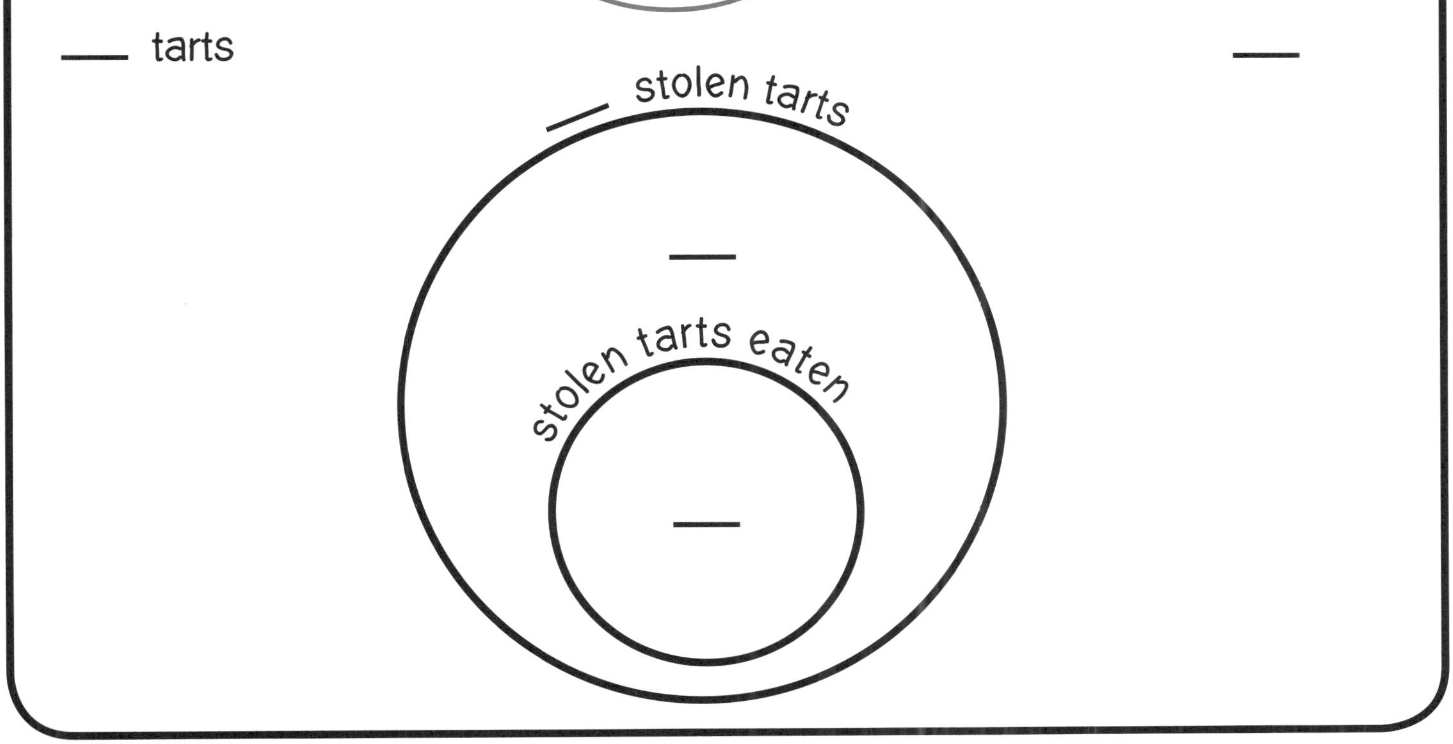

How many stolen tarts were not eaten? ______

Venn Perplexors

The Rhyme

Little Miss Muffet sat on a tuffet,
Eating her curds and whey.
Along came a spider,
And sat down beside her,
And frightened Miss Muffet away.

The Clues

Little Miss Muffet has a snack each morning and afternoon.

Sometimes she has just curds, sometimes just whey, and sometimes curds <u>and</u> whey.

Last week she had whey 11 times.

She had curds and whey 9 times.

Puzzle #14

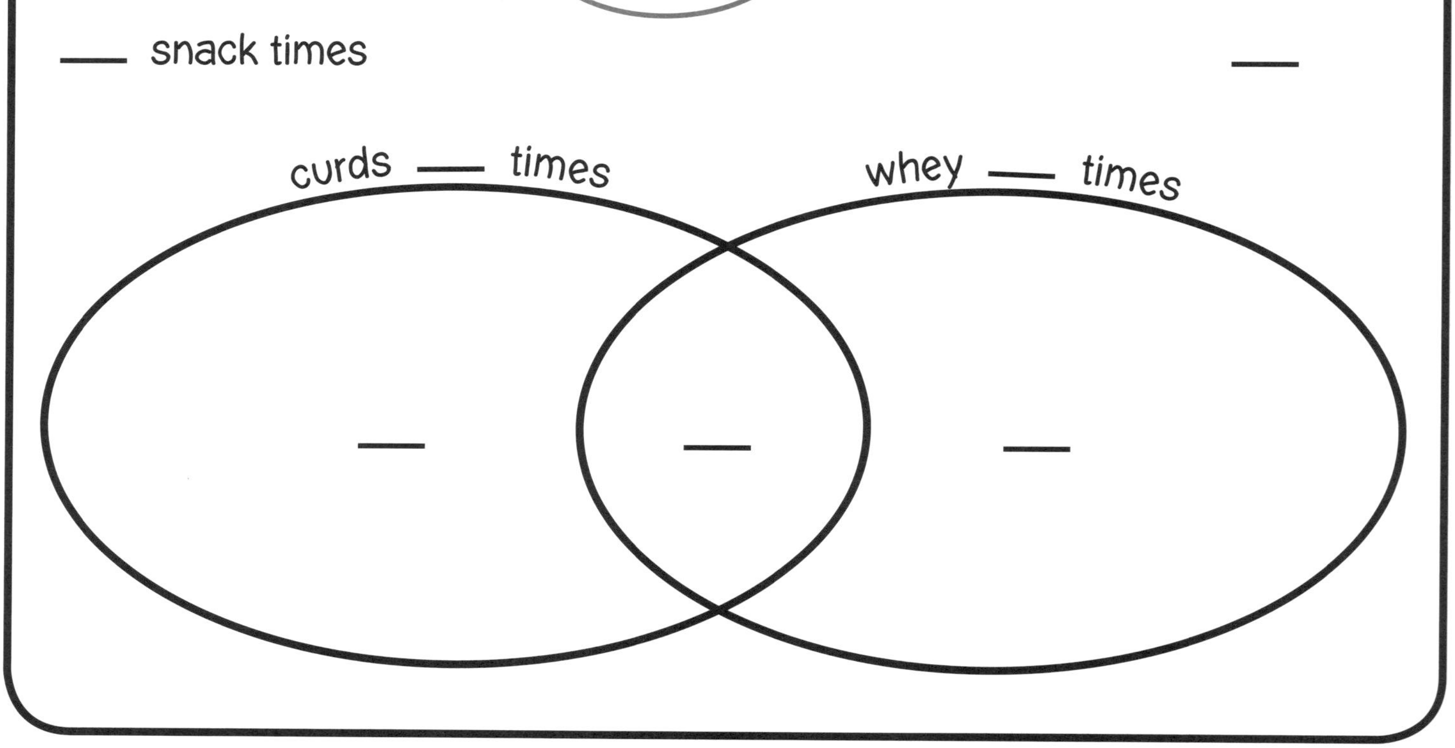

How many times did she have curds? ______

Venn Perplexors

The Rhyme

There was a little girl
Who had a little curl
Right in the middle of her forehead;
When she was good
She was very, very good,
But when she was bad, she was horrid!

The Clues

Unfortunately, yesterday was one of the little girl's really bad days!

Of the 14 hours she was awake, she said horrid things in 10 of them, she did horrid things in 8 of them, and in 6 of them she both said and did horrid things!

Puzzle #15

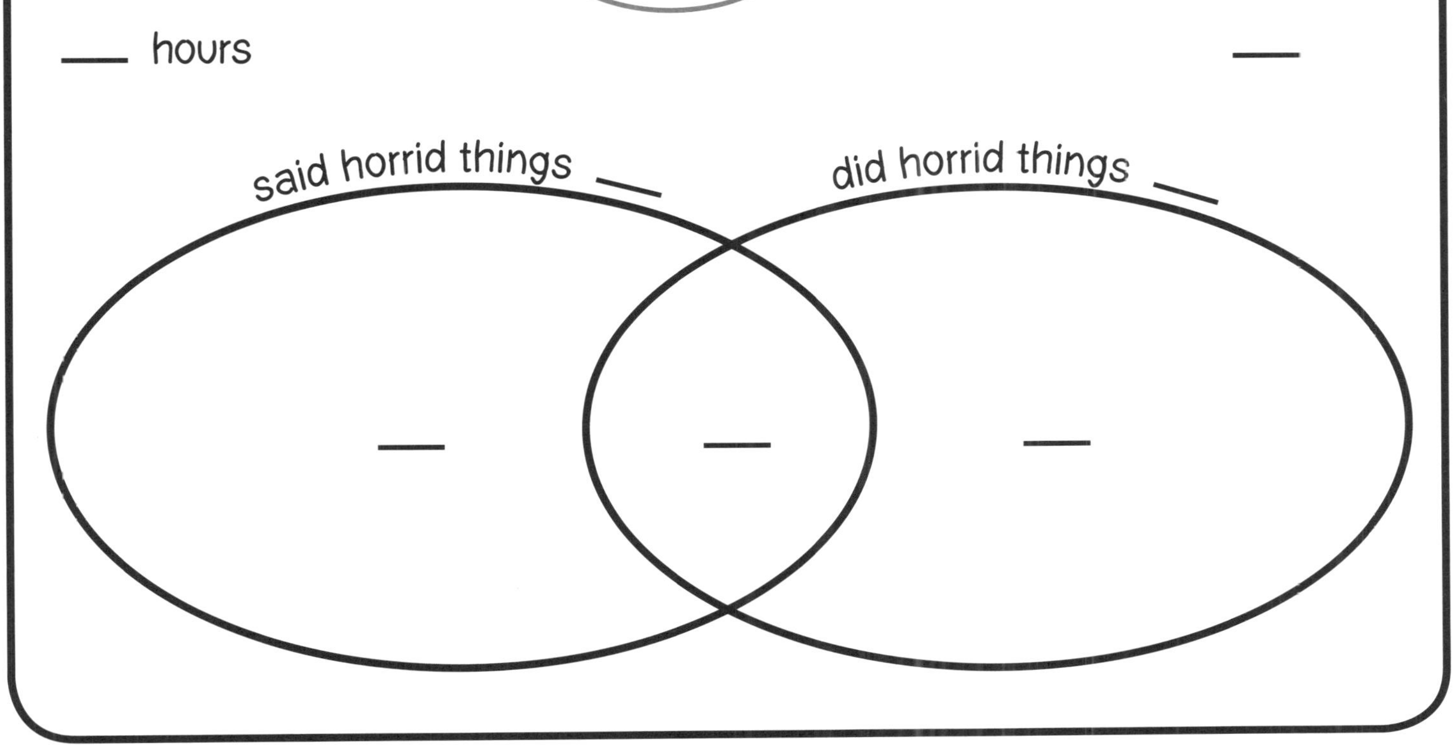

During how many hours was she being very, very good? ______

Venn Perplexors

The Rhyme

Pease porridge hot,
Pease porridge cold,
Pease porridge in the pot
Nine days old.

Some like it hot,
Some like it cold,
Some like it in the pot
Nine days old.

The Clues

Mother Goose's 16 children all like pease porridge.

8 of them like it 9 days old and hot.

3 of them like it 9 days old and cold.

3 like it cold but not 9 days old.

Puzzle #16

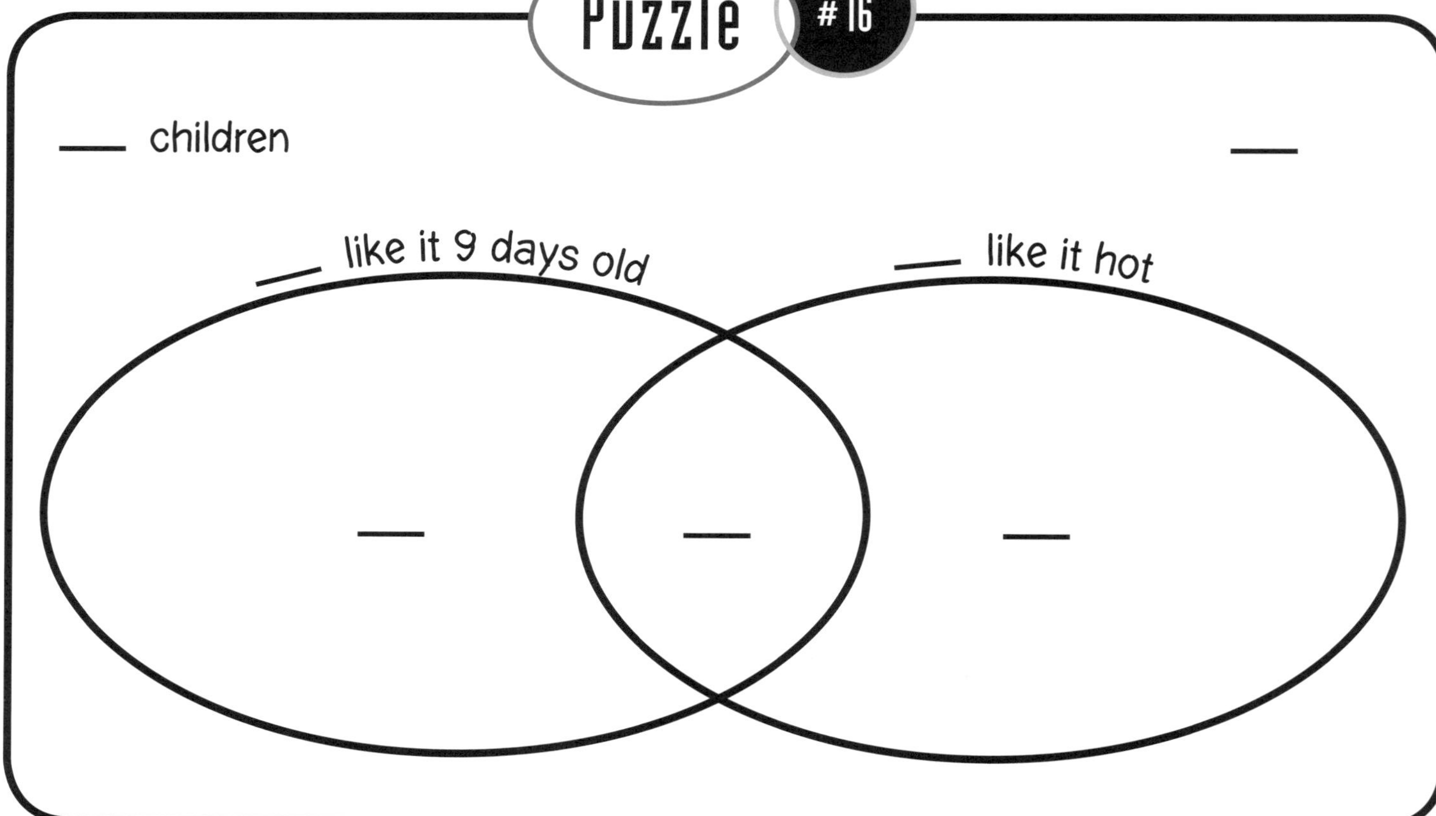

How many like it hot but not 9 days old? ______

Venn Perplexors

The Rhyme

Where, O where,
has my little dog gone?
O where, O where can he be?
With his tail cut short,
And his ears cut long,
O where, O where has he gone?

The Clues

You look at lots and lots of dogs trying to find your little lost dog.

You look at 13 dogs with their ears cut long. You look at 19 dogs with their tails cut short.

11 of the dogs you look at have ears cut long and tails cut short.

24 of the dogs you see have neither long ears nor short tails.

Puzzle #17

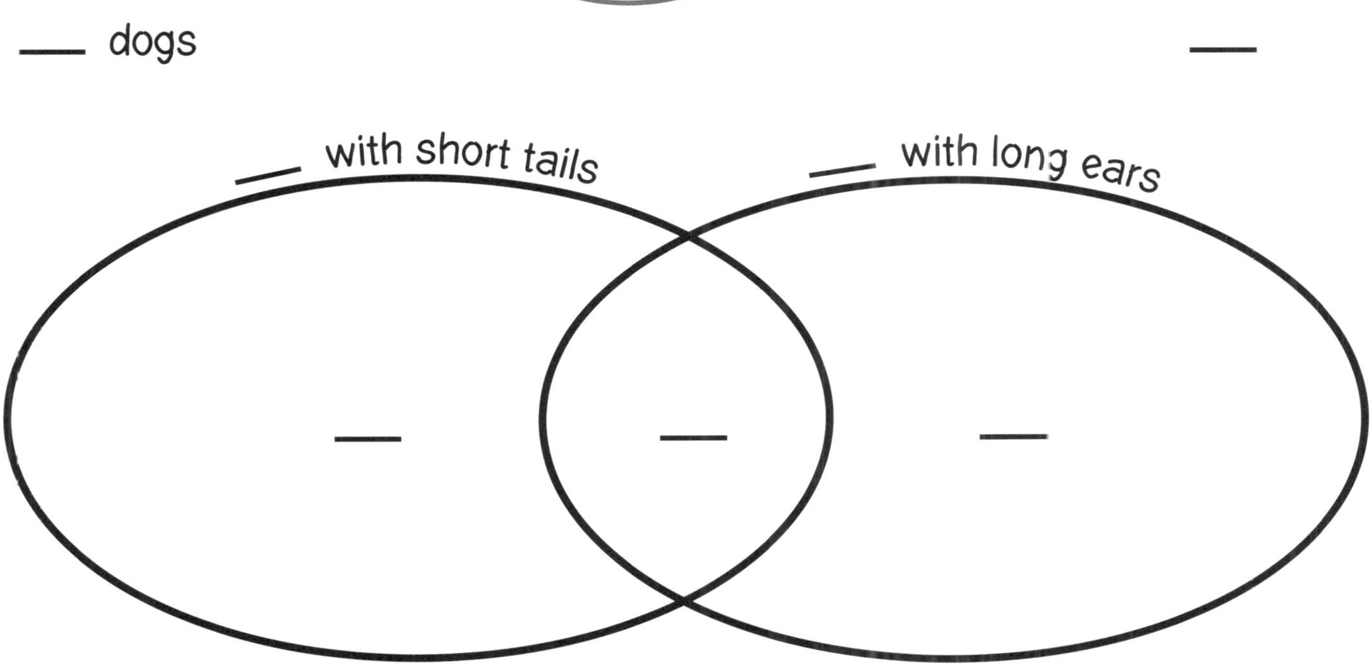

How many dogs did you see? ______

Venn Perplexors

The Rhyme

Peter Piper picked
  a peck of pickled peppers;
A peck of pickled peppers
  Peter Piper picked.
If Peter Piper picked
  a peck of pickled peppers,
Where's the peck of pickled peppers
  Peter Piper picked?

The Clues

Unknown to most people, Peter Piper not only picked pickled peppers, but also pickled cucumbers.

Some of the pecks he picked only had peppers, some only had cucumbers, and some had both. He picked 17 pecks last week.

12 of them had peppers in them. 5 of them had both cucumbers and peppers.

Puzzle #18

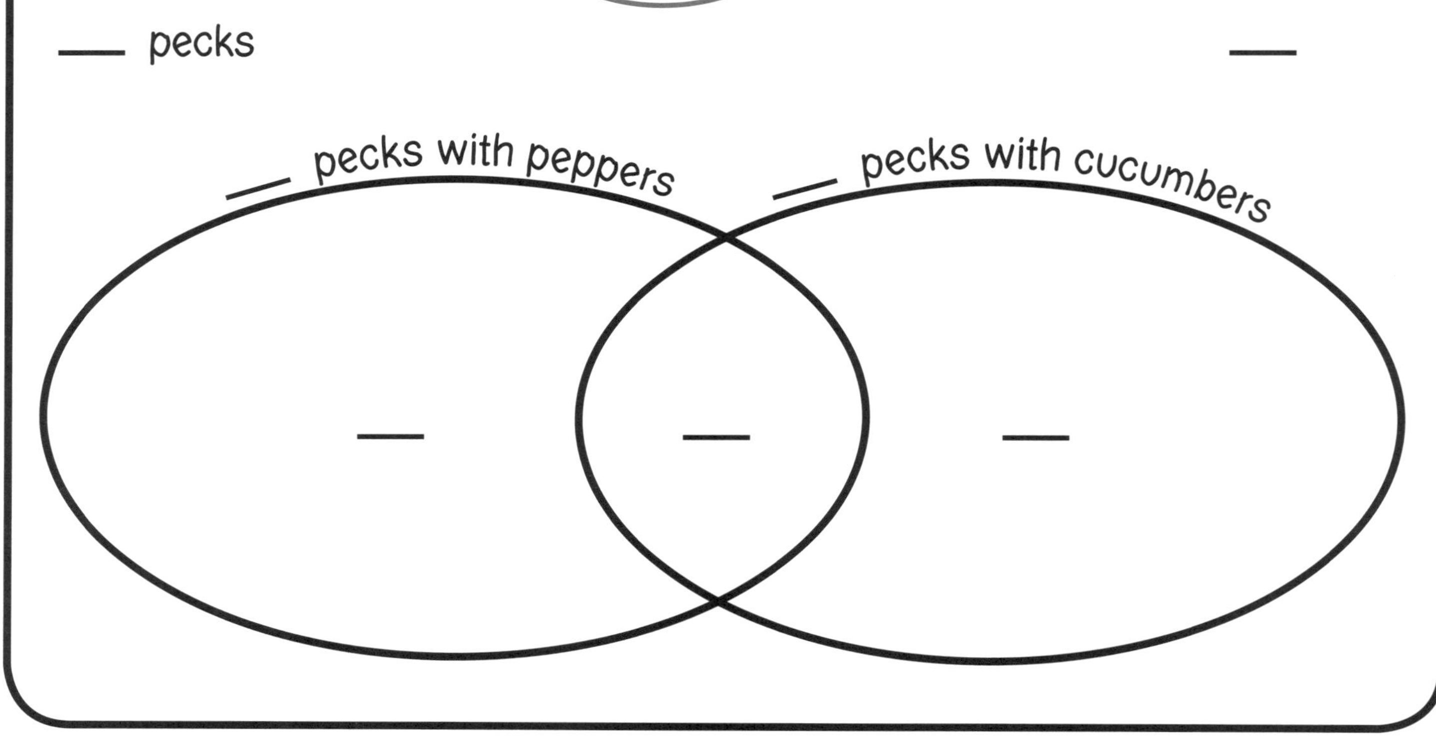

How many had cucumbers in them? _____

 |

Venn Perplexors

The Rhyme

Ride a cockhorse to
 Banbury Cross
To see a fine lady upon a
 white horse;
With rings on her fingers
 And bells on her toes,
She shall have music
 Wherever she goes.

The Clues

The next time you go to Banbury Cross, you notice that the fine lady has really set the fashion!

You see 8 people wearing rings on their fingers and bells on their toes.

You see 7 people wearing bells on their toes but not rings.

A total of 10 people you see have on rings.

You see only 2 people without rings or bells.

Puzzle #19

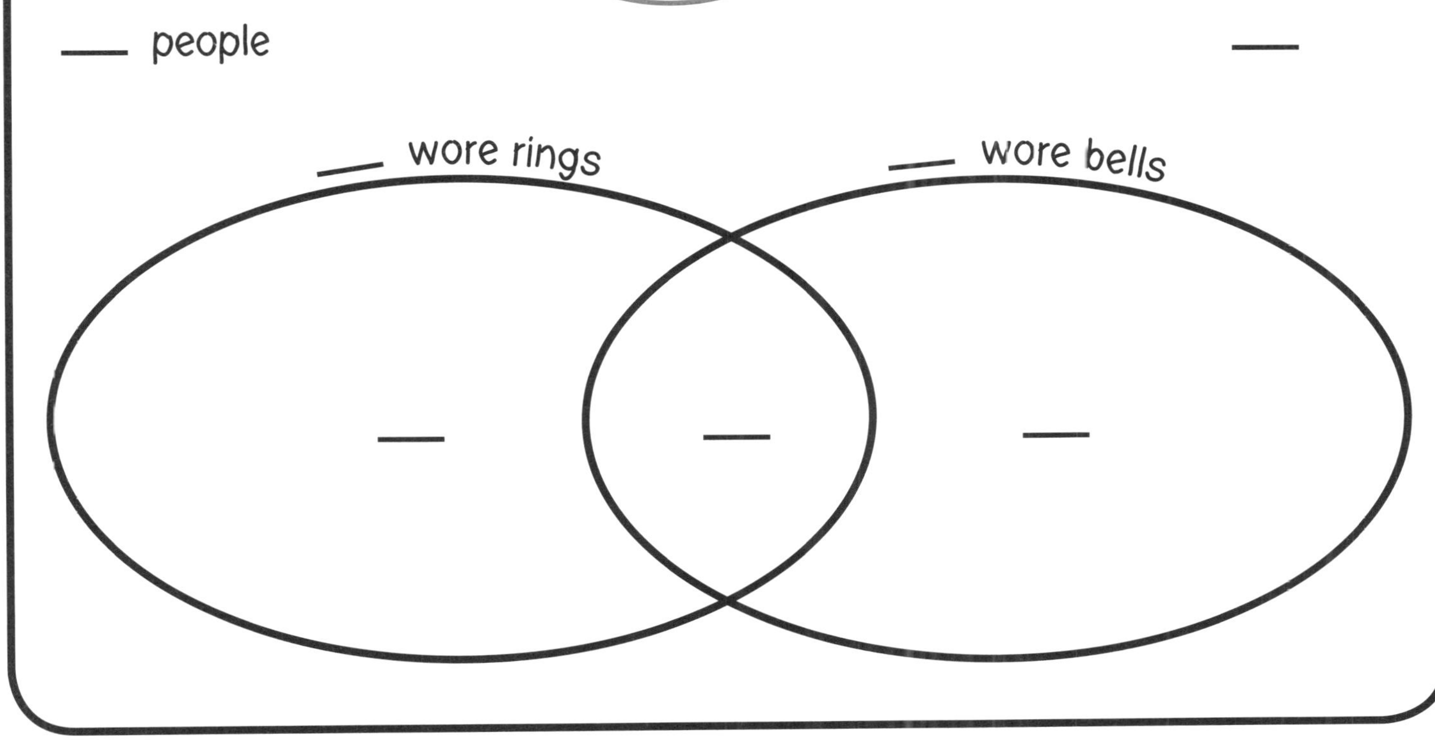

How many people did you see in all? ______

Venn Perplexors

The Rhyme

Hickety Pickety, my black hen,
She lays eggs for gentlemen;
Gentlemen come every day
To see what my fine hen doth lay.
Sometimes nine and sometimes ten,
Hickety Pickety, my black hen.

The Clues

When the gentlemen come to buy Hickety Pickety's eggs, sometimes they want white eggs, sometimes brown, sometimes both, and sometimes they just come and look.

Last week 26 gentlemen came.

21 bought white eggs, 9 bought brown, and 6 bought both.

Puzzle #20

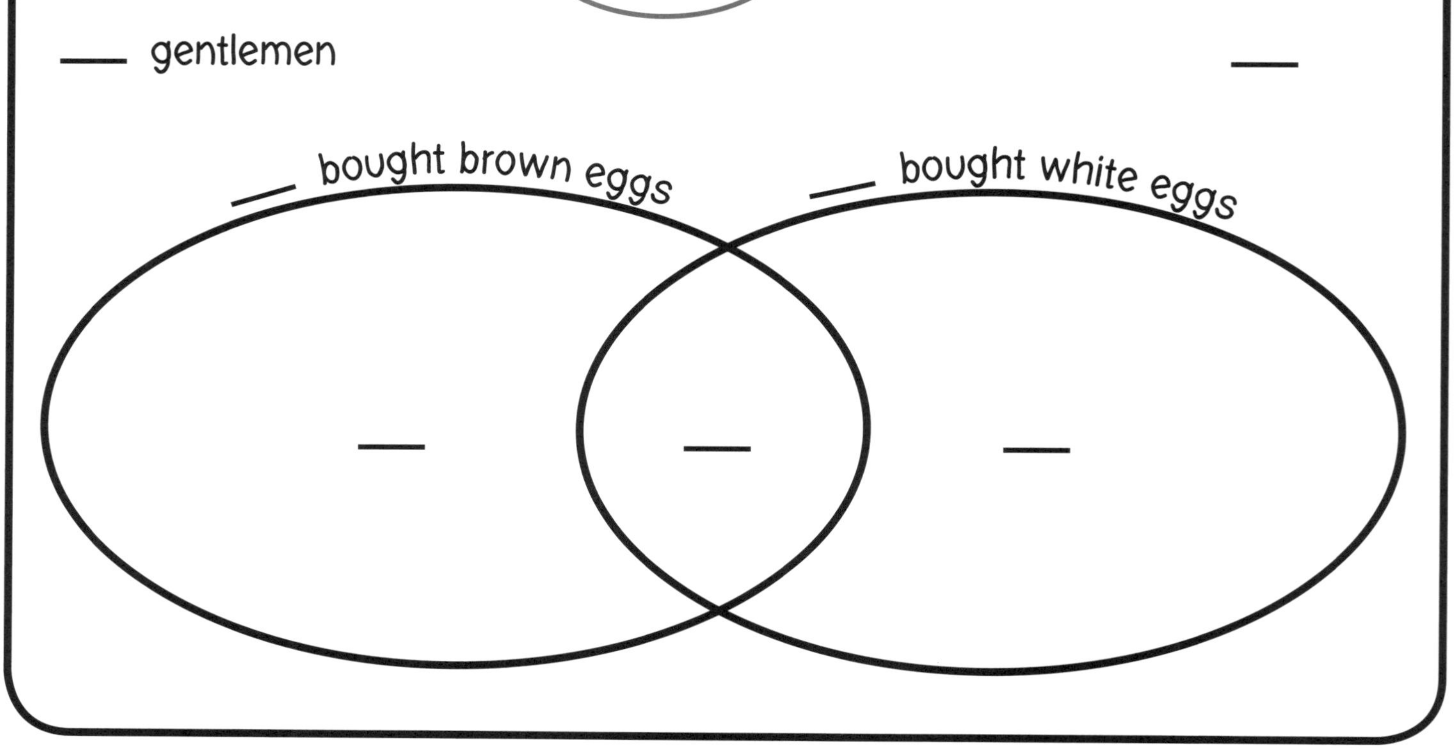

How many didn't buy any eggs? ______

Venn Perplexors

The Rhyme

Baa, baa, black sheep,
Have you any wool?
Yes, sir, yes, sir,
Three bags full.
One for my master,
One for my dame,
And one for the little boy
Who lives down the lane.

The Clues

Sometimes the black sheep doesn't give its wool equally to the master, the dame, and the little boy.

Sometimes the master and dame even have to share their bag between the two of them.

Last year the sheep gave 12 bags.

5 went to the little boy.

The sheep gave to the master 5 times and to the dame 6 times.

Puzzle #21

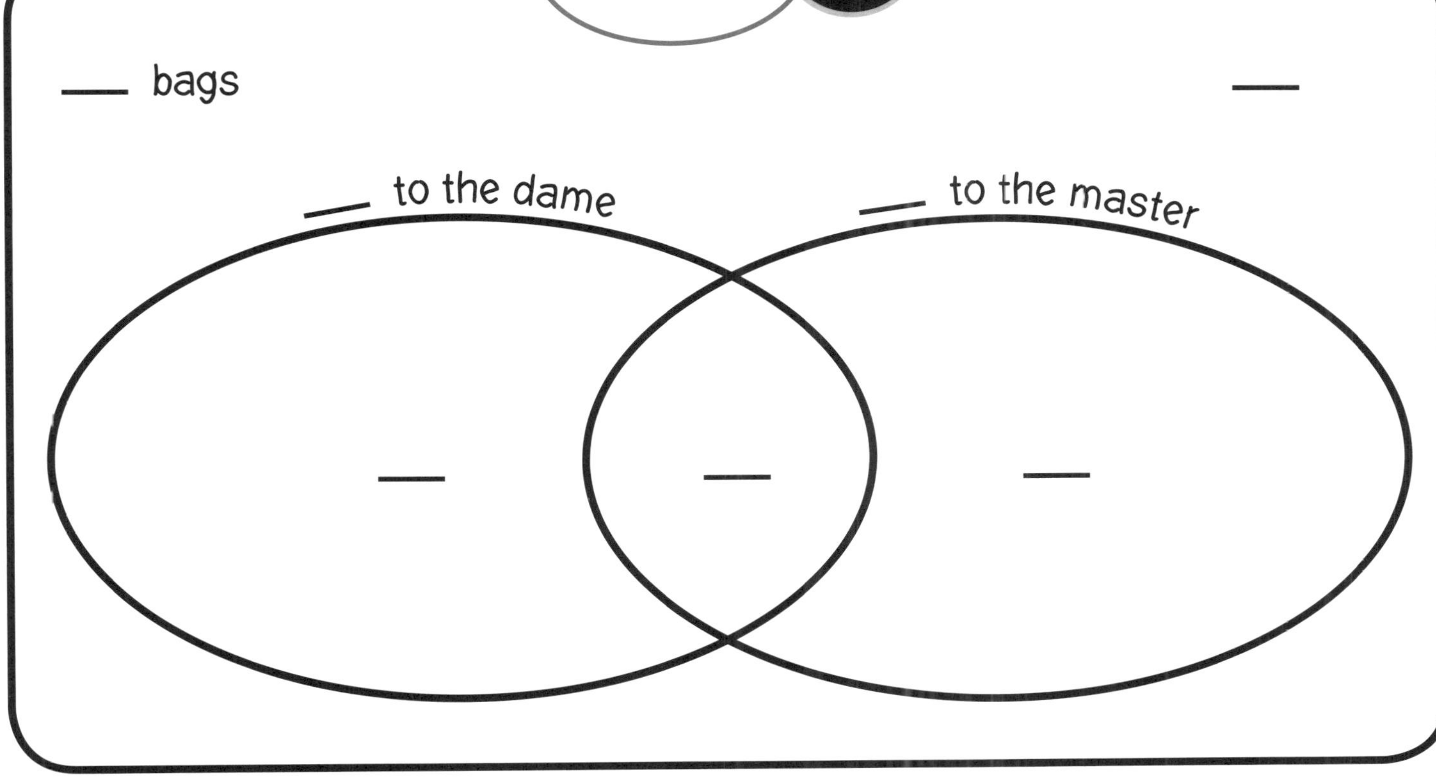

How many times did the master get a bag by himself? ______

Venn Perplexors

The Rhyme

She sells seashells
on the seashore;
The shells that she sells
are seashells I'm sure.
So if she sells seashells
on the seashore,
I'm sure that the shells
are seashore shells.

The Clues

Sheila has been collecting shells all week to sell.

She found 57 scallops (which are her favorites).

She also really likes pink shells. She found 32 of those.

48 of the shells weren't pink or scallops.

Puzzle #22

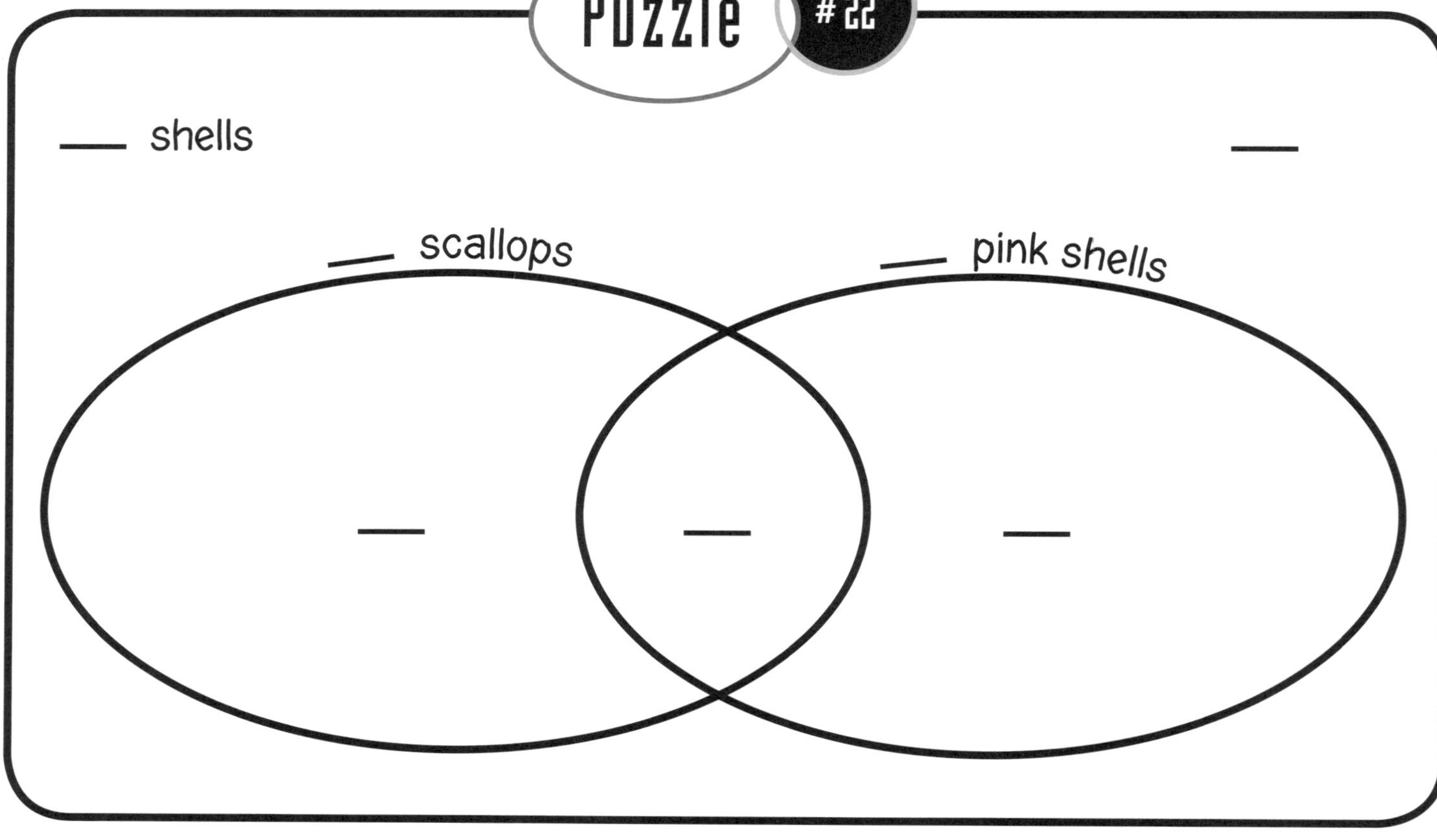

If Sheila found 114 shells in all, how many of her scallops weren't pink?

___

 |

Venn Perplexors

The Rhyme

Wee Willie Winkie
runs through the town,
Upstairs and downstairs
in his nightgown,
Rapping at the window,
Crying through the lock,
Are all the children in their beds?
For now it's eight o'clock.

The Clues

There are 41 children in the town.

When Wee Willie runs through at 8 o'clock checking on them, he finds only 32 of them in bed.

34 of the children have brushed their teeth.

3 naughty children have not brushed their teeth or gone to bed!

Puzzle #23

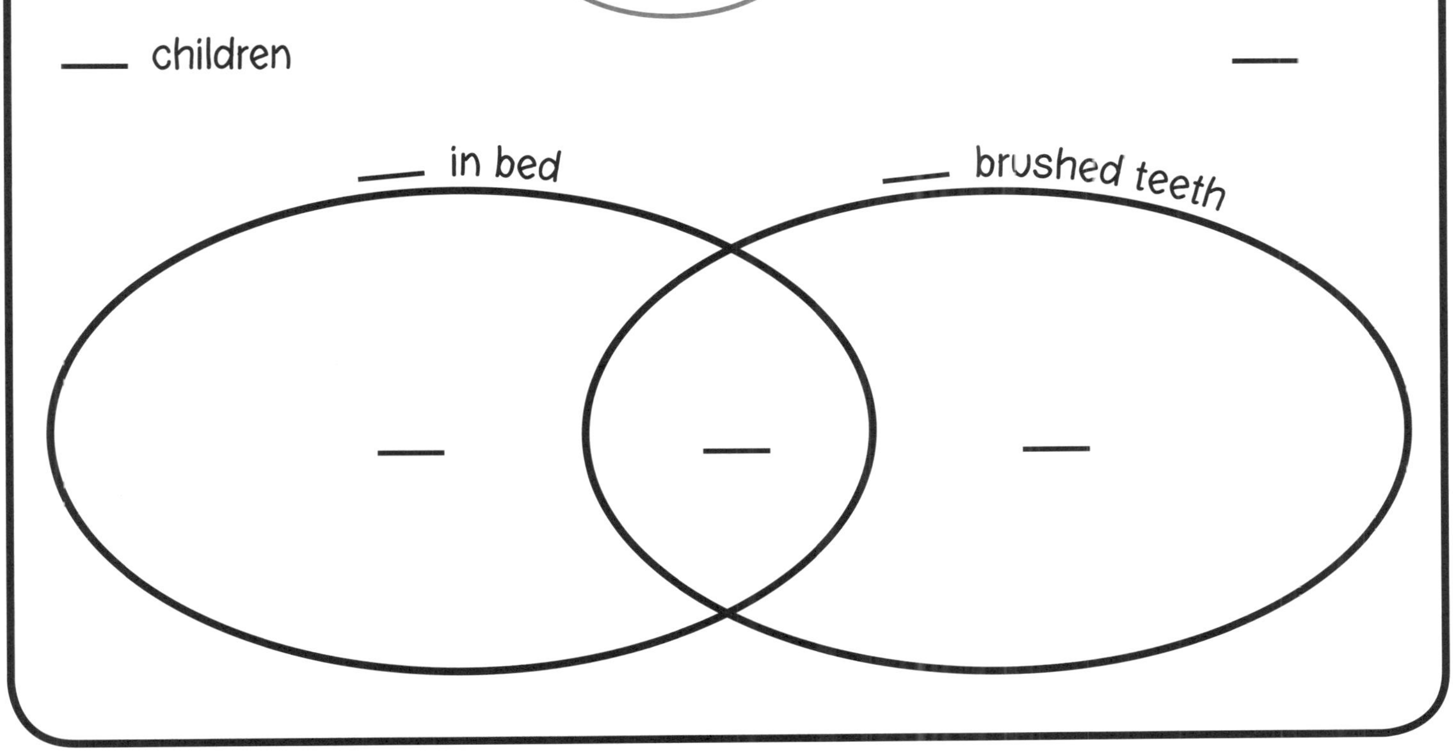

How many need to get out of bed to go brush their teeth? ______

Venn Perplexors

The Rhyme

The lion and the unicorn
Were fighting for the crown;
The lion beat the unicorn
All round about the town.

Some gave them white bread,
And some gave them brown;
Some gave them plum-cake,
And sent them out of town.

The Clues

8 of the townspeople gave the lion and the unicorn white bread.

4 gave them just brown bread.

3 gave them both brown and white bread.

2 gave them only plum-cake.

Puzzle #24

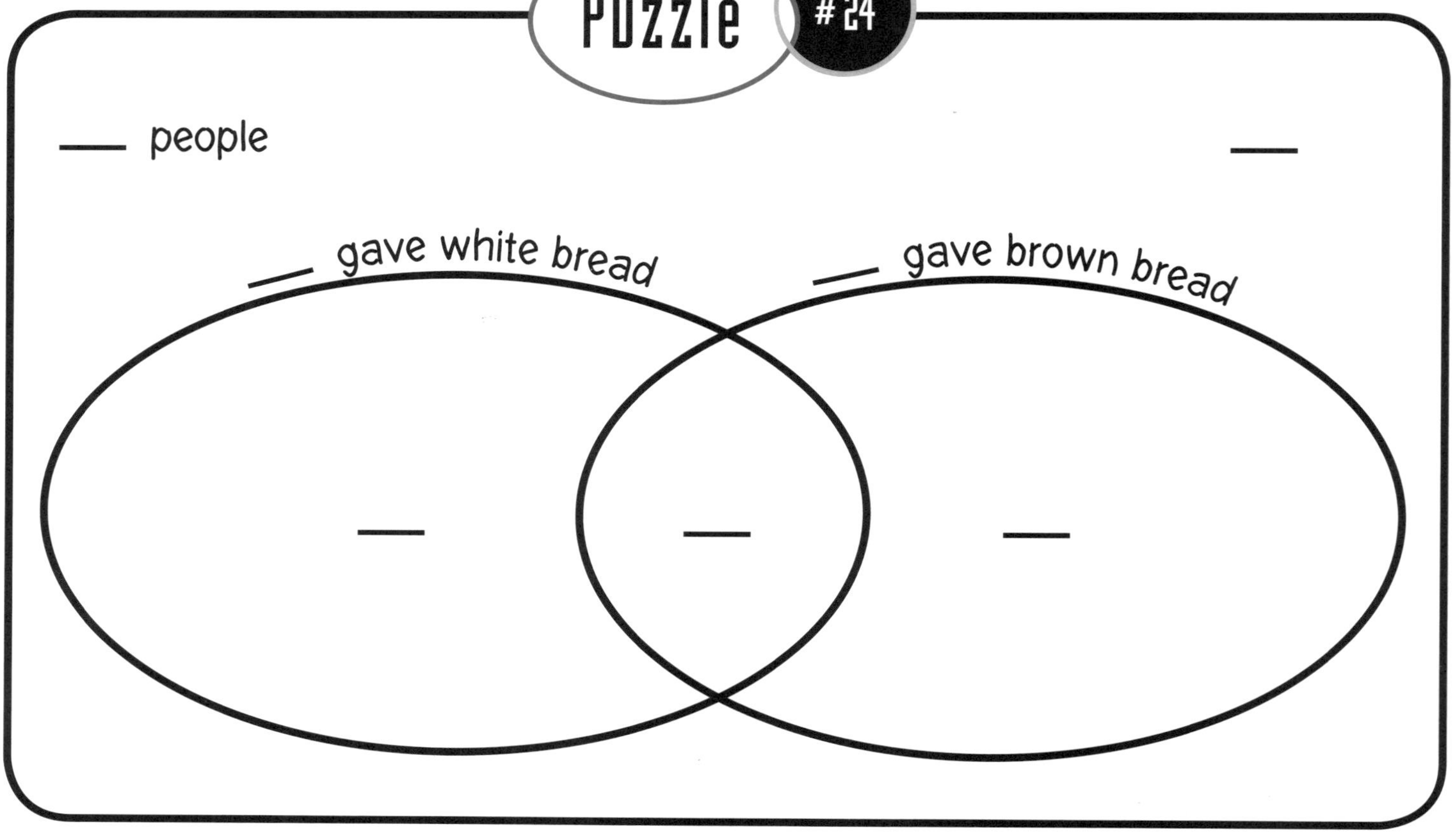

What fraction of the people who gave the lion and unicorn food, gave them brown bread? ______

Venn Perplexors

The Rhyme

One misty, moisty morning,
When cloudy was the weather,
I chanced to meet an old man
Clothed all in leather.

Clothed all in leather,
With cap under his chin.
How do you do, and how do you do,
And how do you do again?

The Clues

As it happens, the old man goes out every morning, regardless of the weather.

Last month (March), 19 of the days were wet and cold.

Altogether there were 27 cold days and 21 wet days.

Puzzle #25

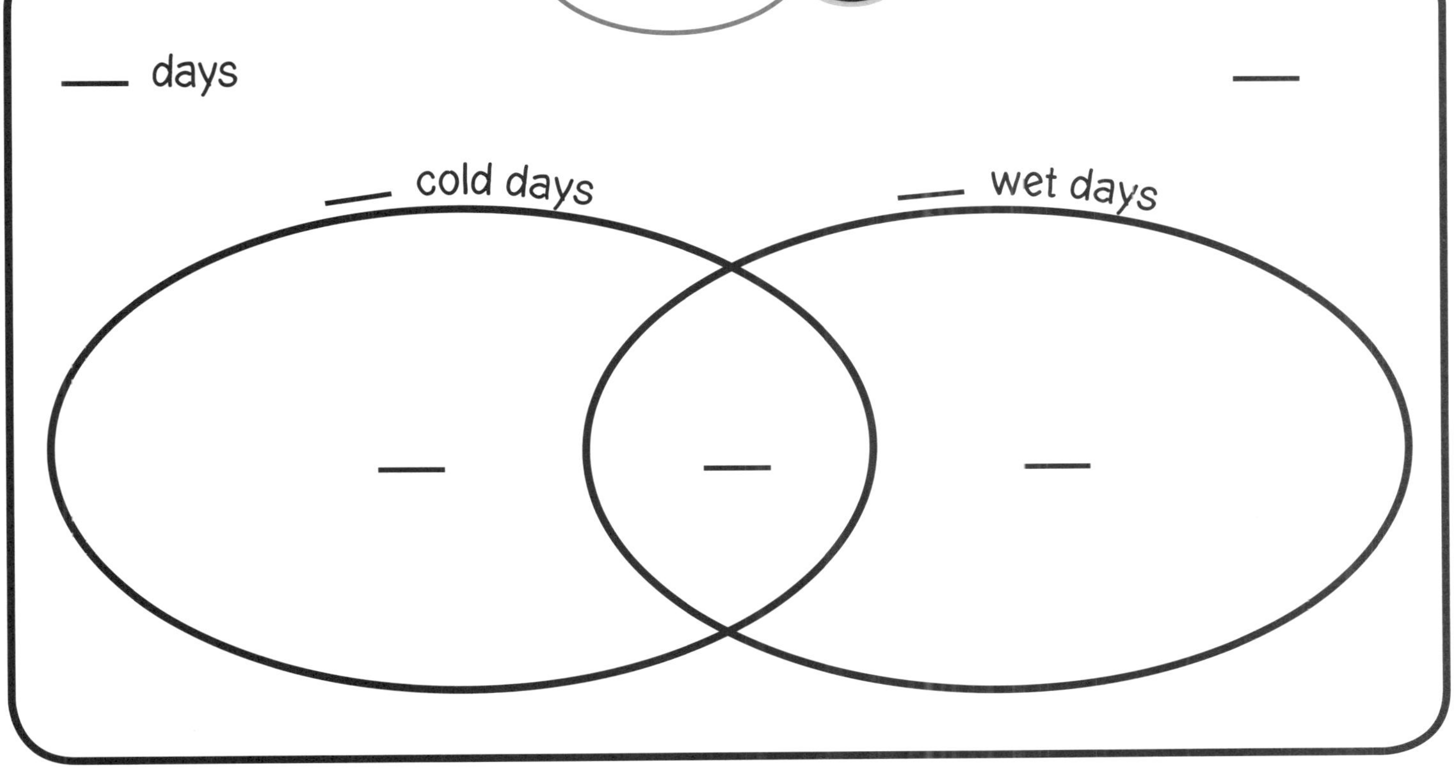

How many days were neither wet nor cold? ______

Venn Perplexors

The Rhyme

Diddle diddle dumpling, my son John,
Went to bed with his stockings on;
One shoe off and one shoe on,
Diddle diddle dumpling, my son John.

The Clues

John was in bed asleep for 10 hours.

After 6 hours he kicked off his shoe.

He was dreaming for 7 hours of the night.

For 1 hour he wasn't dreaming and he didn't have his shoe on.

Puzzle #26

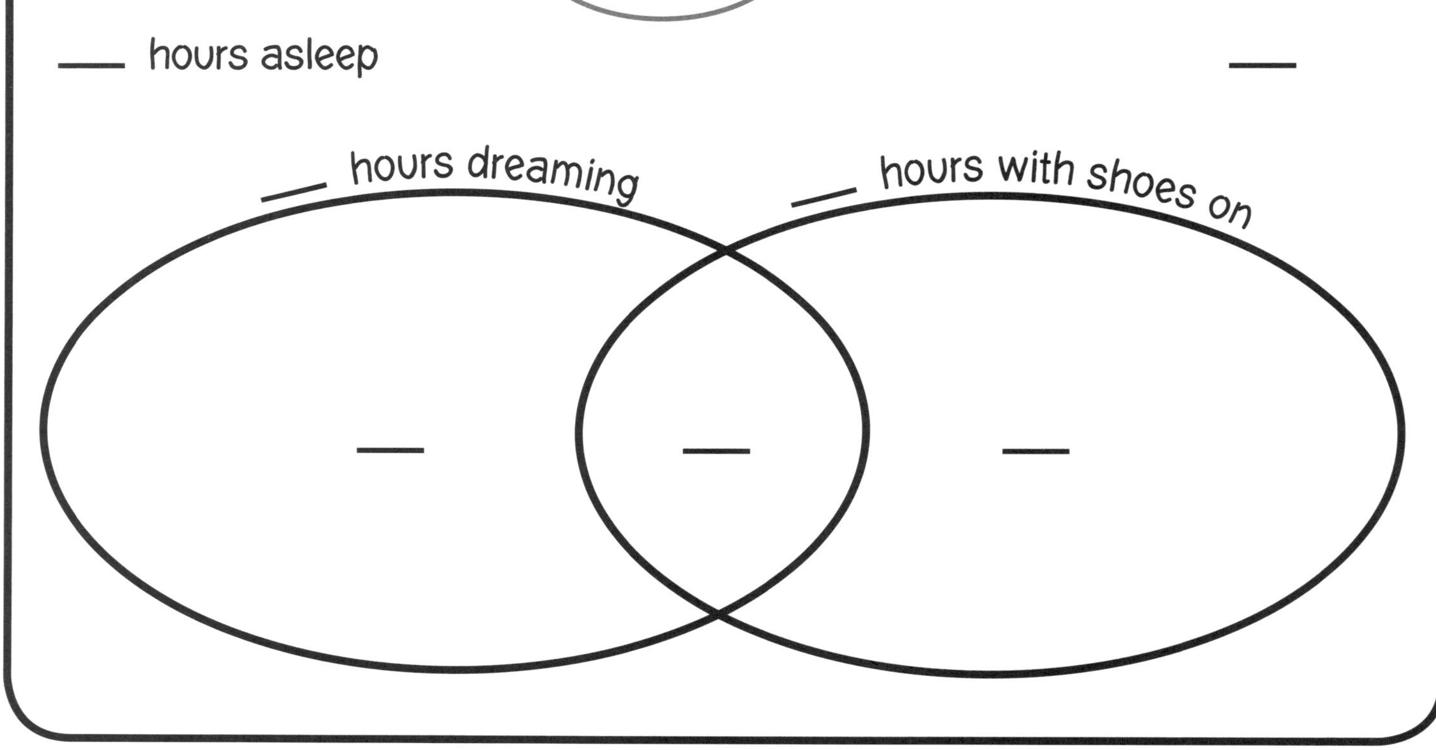

How many hours did John dream without his shoe on? ______

Venn Perplexors

The Rhyme

Three young rats with black felt hats,
Three young cats with white straw flats*,
Three young dogs with turned-up tails,
Three young ducks with bridal veils.

Went out to walk with two young pigs
In satin vests and curly wigs.
But suddenly it chanced to rain
And so they all went home again.

The Clues

Read the nursery rhyme, count how many animals belong in each set or subset, and write the numbers in the diagram below.

Puzzle # 27

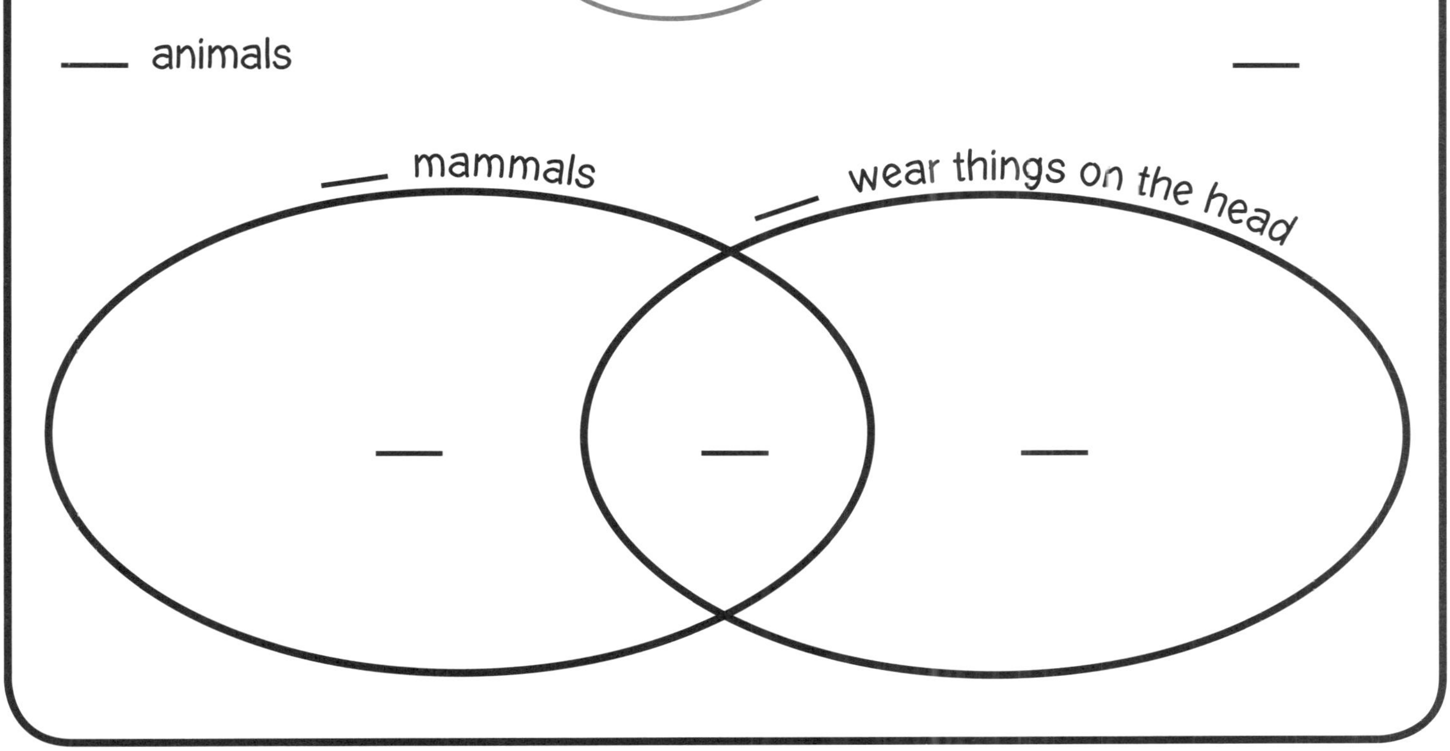

*Note: "flats" are shoes with very low heels.

Venn Perplexors

The Rhyme

Buttons, a farthing a pair!
Come, who will buy them of me?
They're round and sound and pretty
And fit for the girls of the city.
Come, who will buy them of me?
Buttons, a farthing a pair!

The Clues

The vendor has 100 buttons for sale.

70 buttons are colored.

42 buttons have 4 holes.

16 are white and do not have 4 holes.

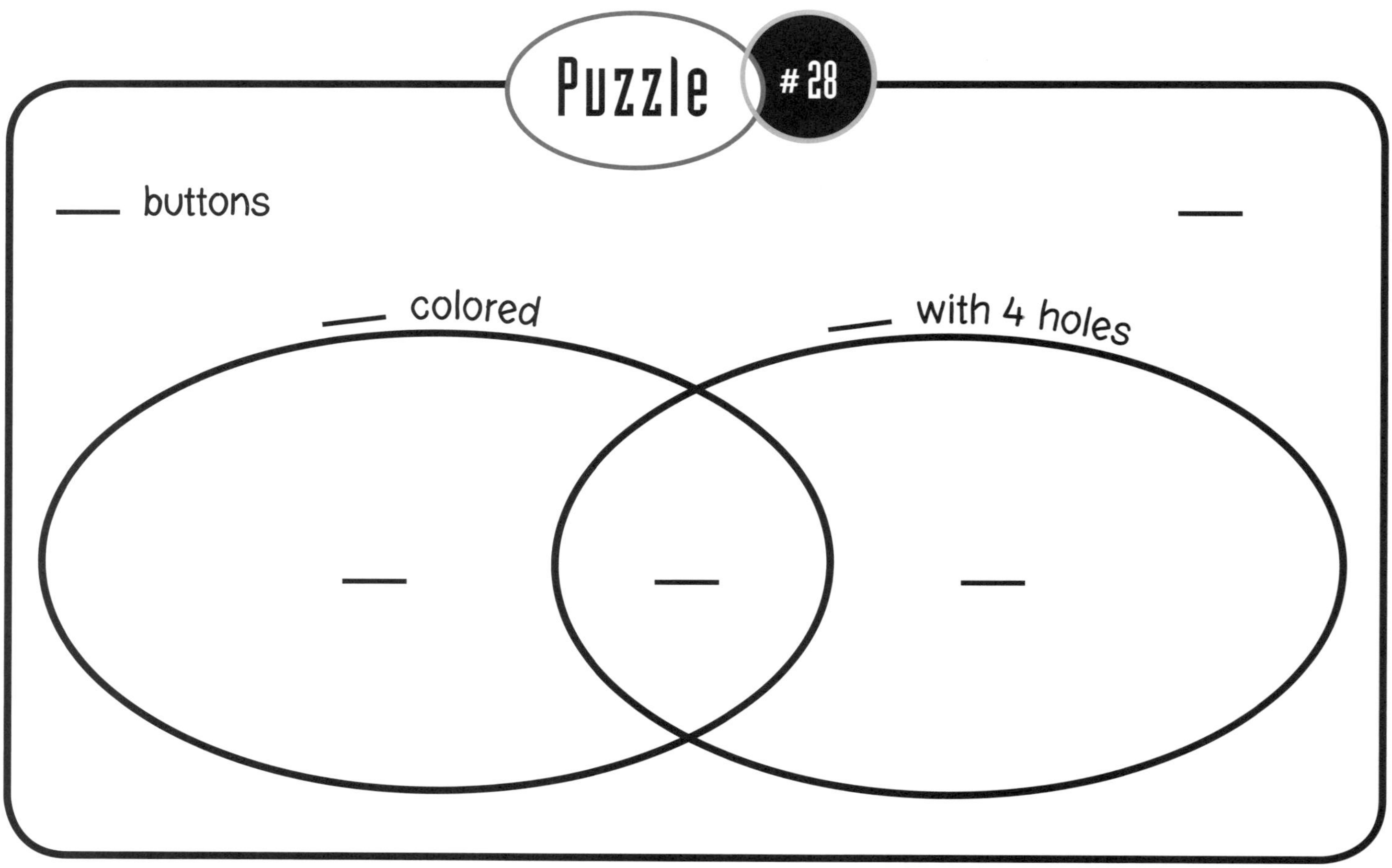

If you want a 4-holed, colored button, from how many will you be able to choose? ______

 |

Venn Perplexors

The Rhyme

Mary, Mary, quite contrary,
How does your garden grow?
With silver bells and cockle shells
And pretty maids all in a row.

The Clues

Mary's garden was very strange indeed with silver bells, cockle shells, and pretty maids.

Each day in June she worked on weeding either the silver bells, pretty maids, or both, or she worked on rearranging the cockle shells.

On 11 days she weeded just bells.

On 7 days she weeded just maids.

On 5 days she rearranged cockle shells.

Puzzle #29

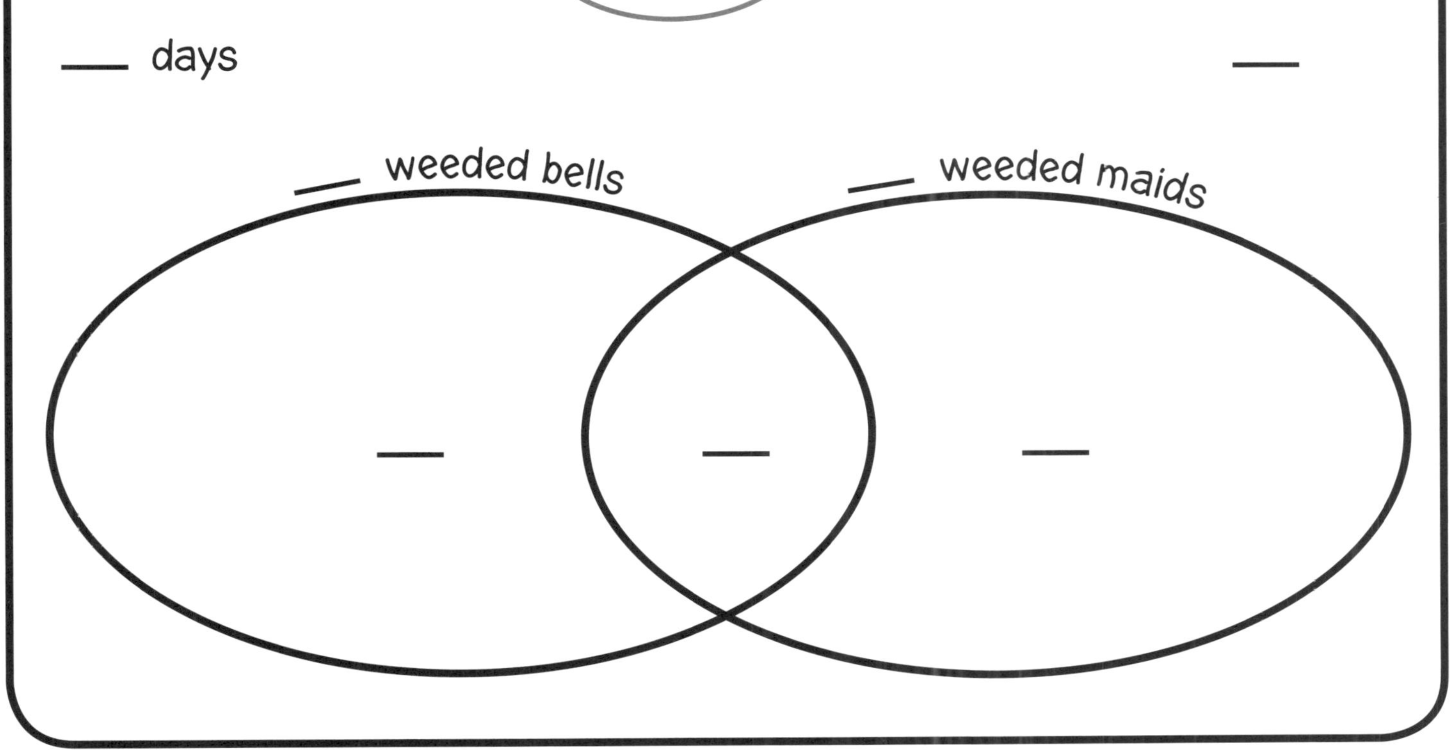

On how many days altogether did she weed the silver bells? ______

Venn Perplexors

The Rhyme

Old King Cole
Was a merry old soul,
And a merry old soul was he;
He called for his pipe,
And he called for his bowl,
And he called for his fiddlers three.

The Clues

Old King Cole liked to have his fiddlers play for him 3 times a day, at the end of each meal.

Some of these times he would call for his pipe, sometimes his bowl, sometimes both, and sometimes neither.

Last week he called for both his pipe and bowl 4 times, his pipe 7 times, and his bowl without his pipe 12 times.

Puzzle # 30

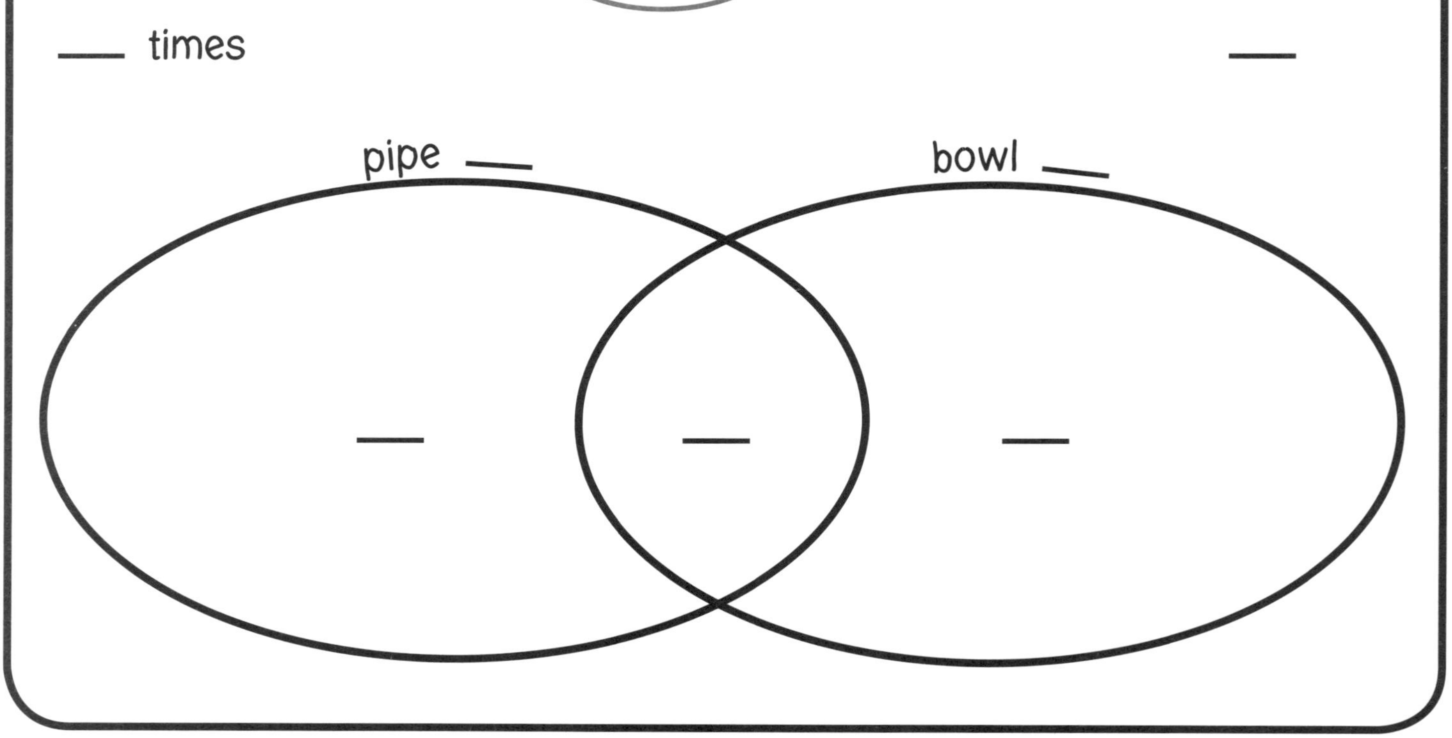

How many times did he call for neither? ___

Venn Perplexors

The Rhyme

Old Mother Hubbard
Went to the cupboard
To get her poor dog a bone;
But when she got there
The cupboard was bare,
And so the poor dog had none.

The Clues

On the last day of May, the cupboard was bare, so old Mother Hubbard's dog got nothing.

But on all the rest of the days of May he got either bones, canned dog food, or both.

He got both on 10 days and on 9 he got just dog food.

Puzzle #31

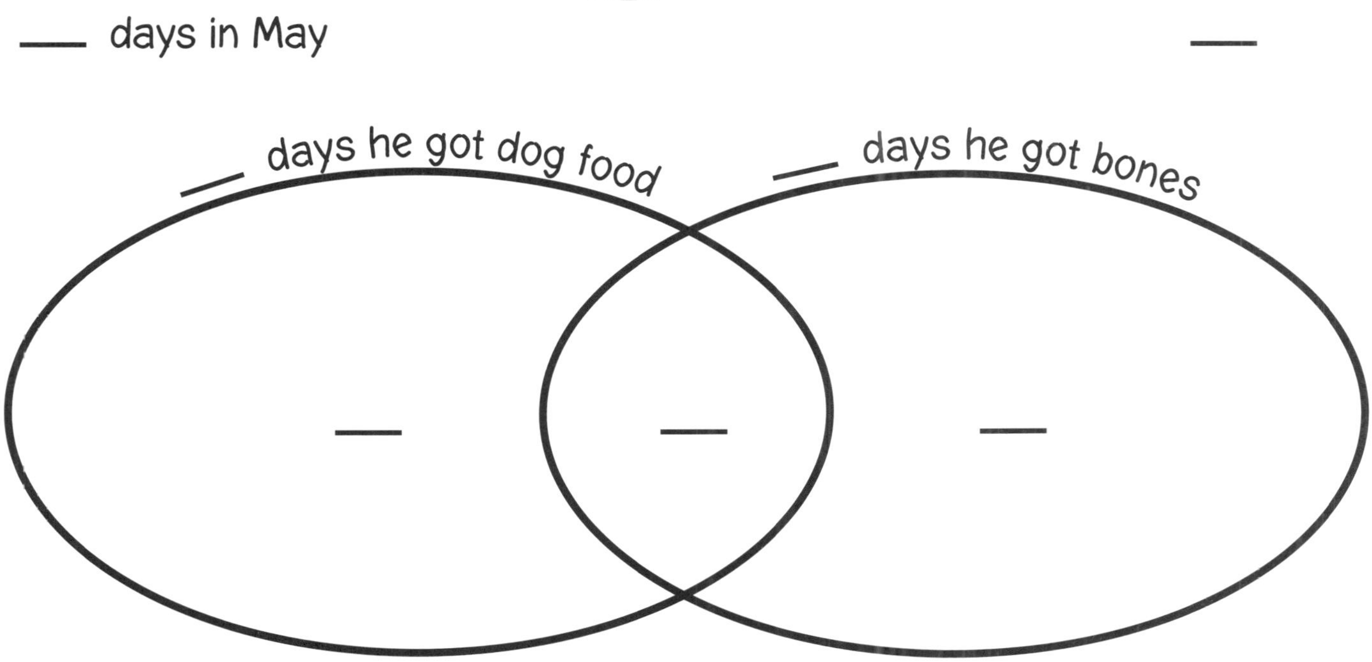

On how many days did he get bones? ______

Venn Perplexors

The Rhyme

Hot cross buns!
Hot cross buns!
One a penny, two a penny,
Hot cross buns!
If you have no daughters,
Give them to your sons.
One a penny, two a penny,
Hot cross buns!

The Clues

Some of the hot cross buns for sale have both nuts and raisins inside. They cost one for a penny.

The others have <u>either</u> nuts or raisins. They cost two for a penny.

You've decided to buy 20 buns for your sons. 12 of them have raisins. 6 have both raisins and nuts

Puzzle #32

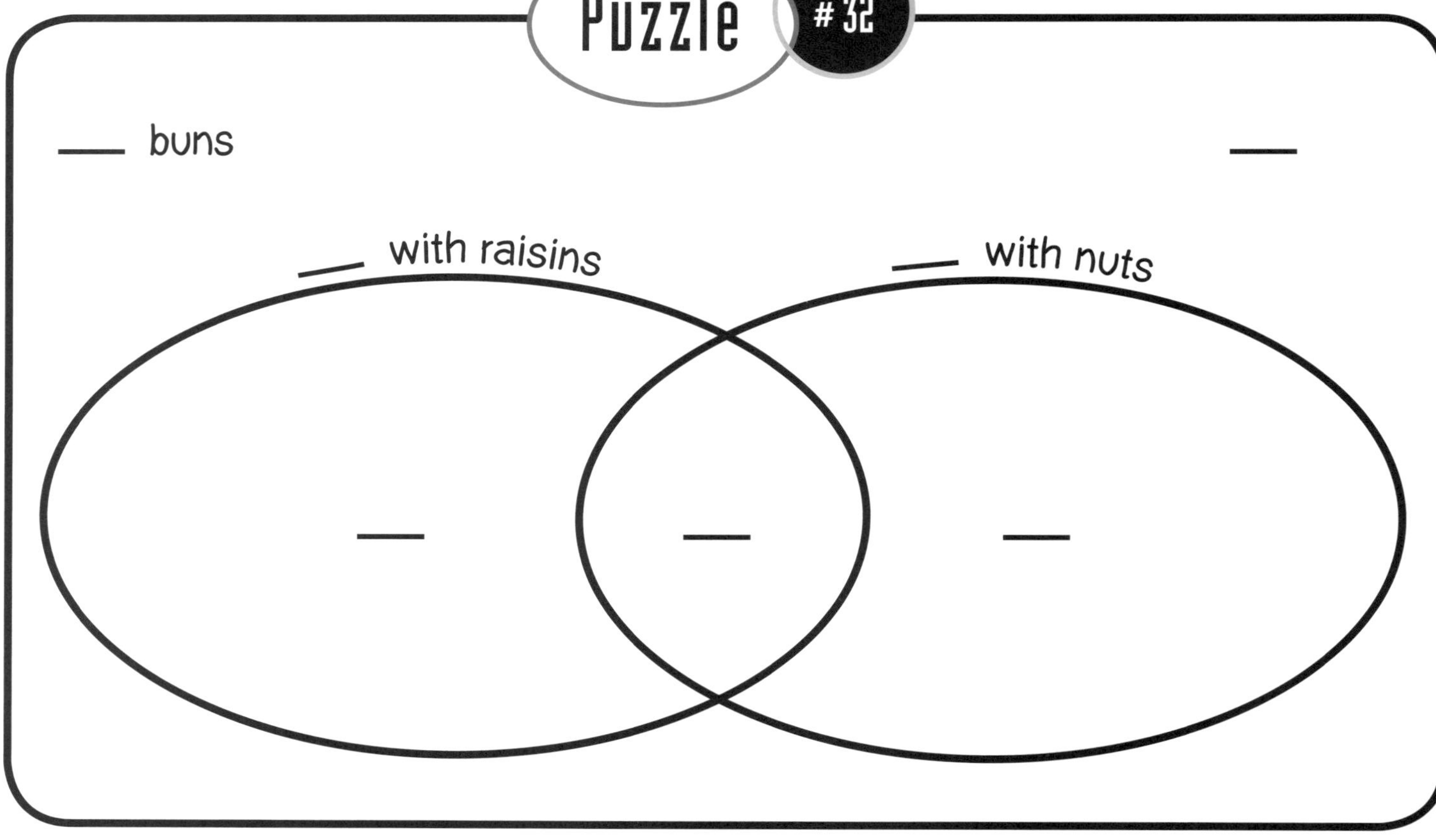

How much do the 20 buns cost? ______

Venn Perplexors

The Rhyme

Hickory, dickory dock!
The mouse ran up the clock.
The clock struck one,
The mouse ran down,
Hickory, dickory dock!

The Clues

The twin mice, Hickory and Dickory, share the job of running up the clock whenever it strikes the hour.

And sometimes, just for fun, they both run up when it strikes.

Yesterday Dickory ran up 9 times by himself and the 2 mice ran up 4 times together.

Puzzle # 33

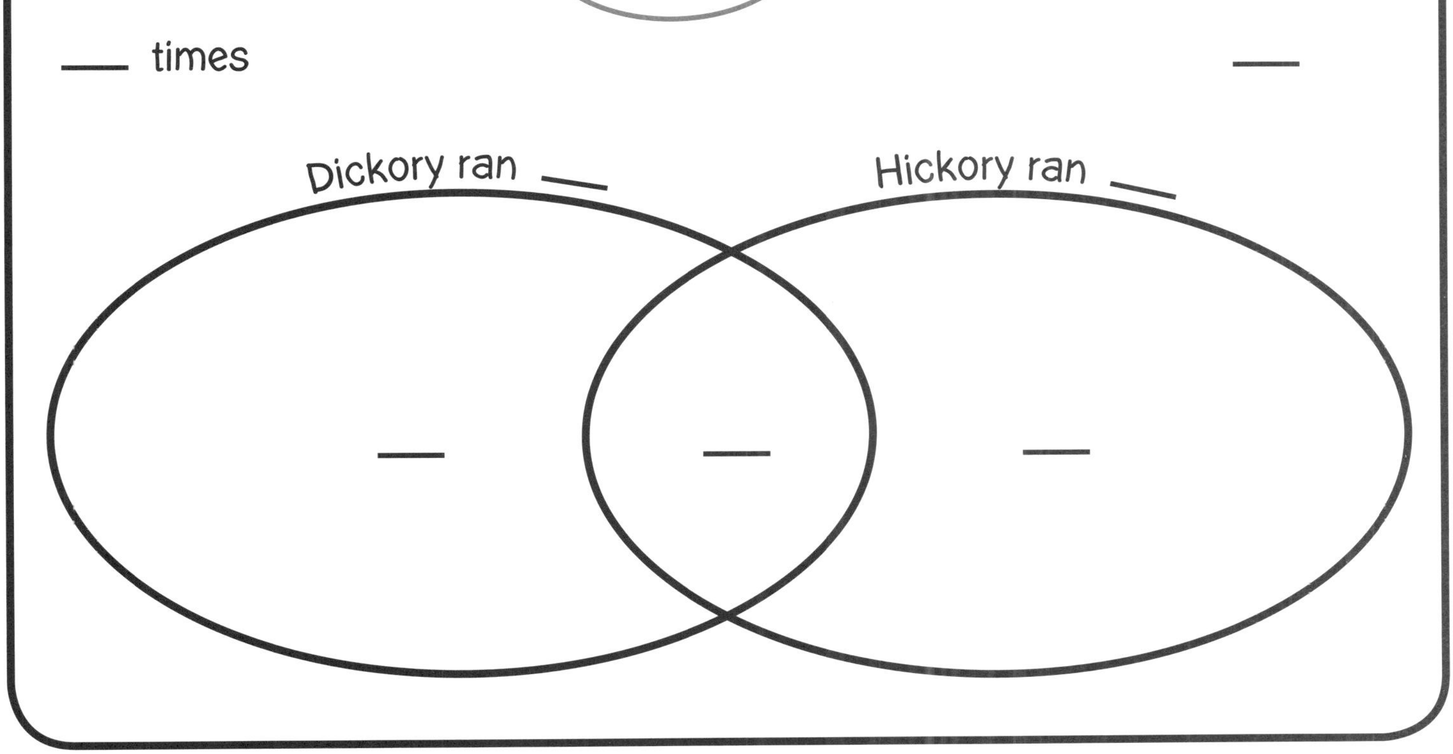

How many more times did Hickory run up than Dickory? ______

Venn Perplexors

The Rhyme

Jack and Jill went up the hill
To fetch a pail of water;
Jack fell down and broke his crown,
And Jill came tumbling after.

The Clues

Last year (which wasn't a leap year) Jack and Jill had lots of trouble fetching the water!

They went up the hill every day.

On 139 days they both fell down.

Jill fell a total of 211 days and Jack fell a total of 243.

Puzzle #34

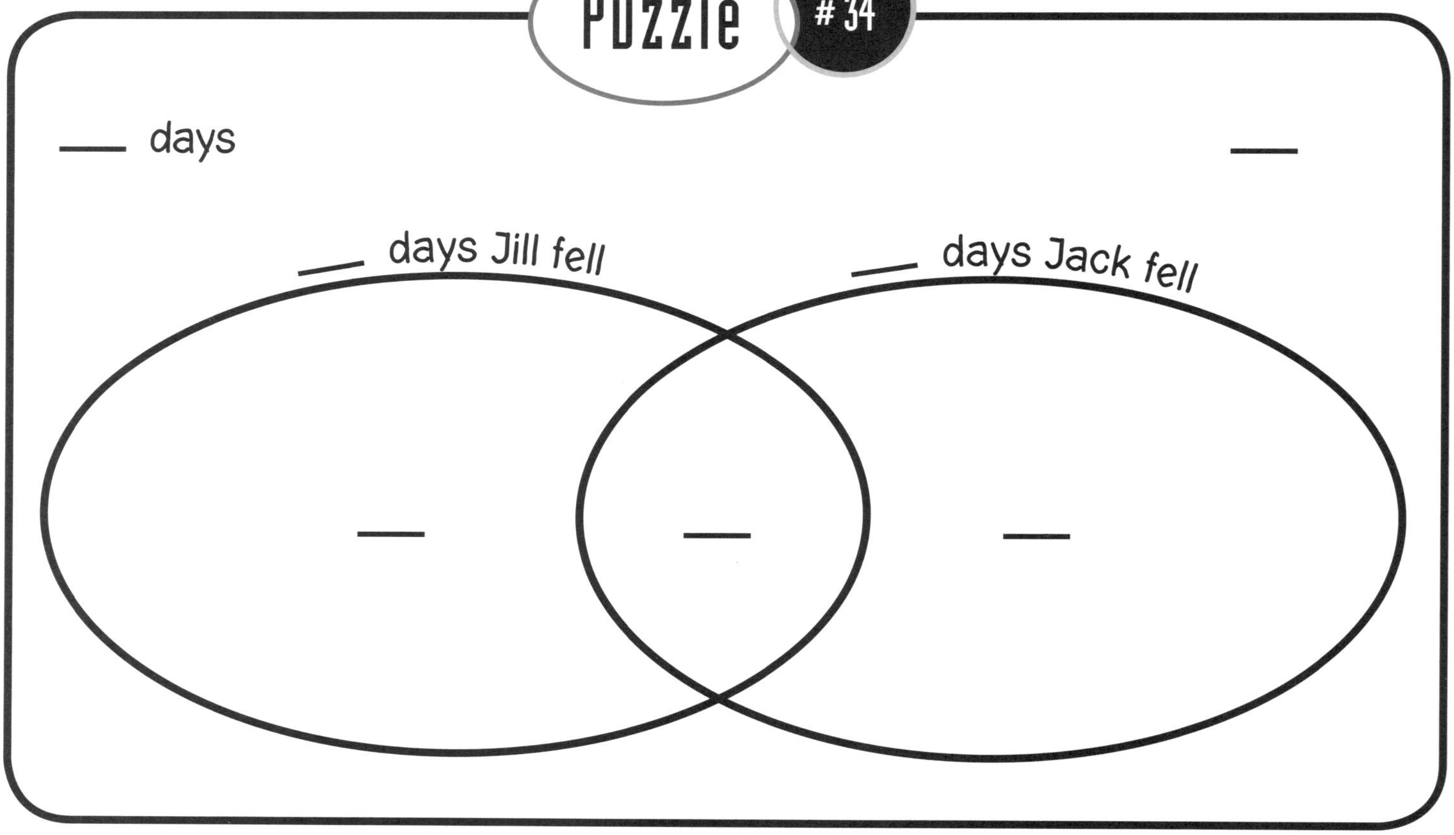

? On how many days did neither fall? ______

Venn Perplexors

The Rhyme

Three little kittens lost their mittens,
And they began to cry,
Oh, mother dear, we sadly fear
Our mittens we have lost.

What! Lost your mittens,
you naughty kittens!
Then you shall have no pie.
Me-ow, me-ow, me-ow, me-ow.
No, you shall have no pie.

The Clues

The 3 little kittens lost 12 mittens.

They lost some in the morning and some in the afternoon.

They lost some in the meadow and some in the yard.

4 were lost in the morning, 3 in the yard in the afternoon, and 7 in the meadow.

Puzzle # 35

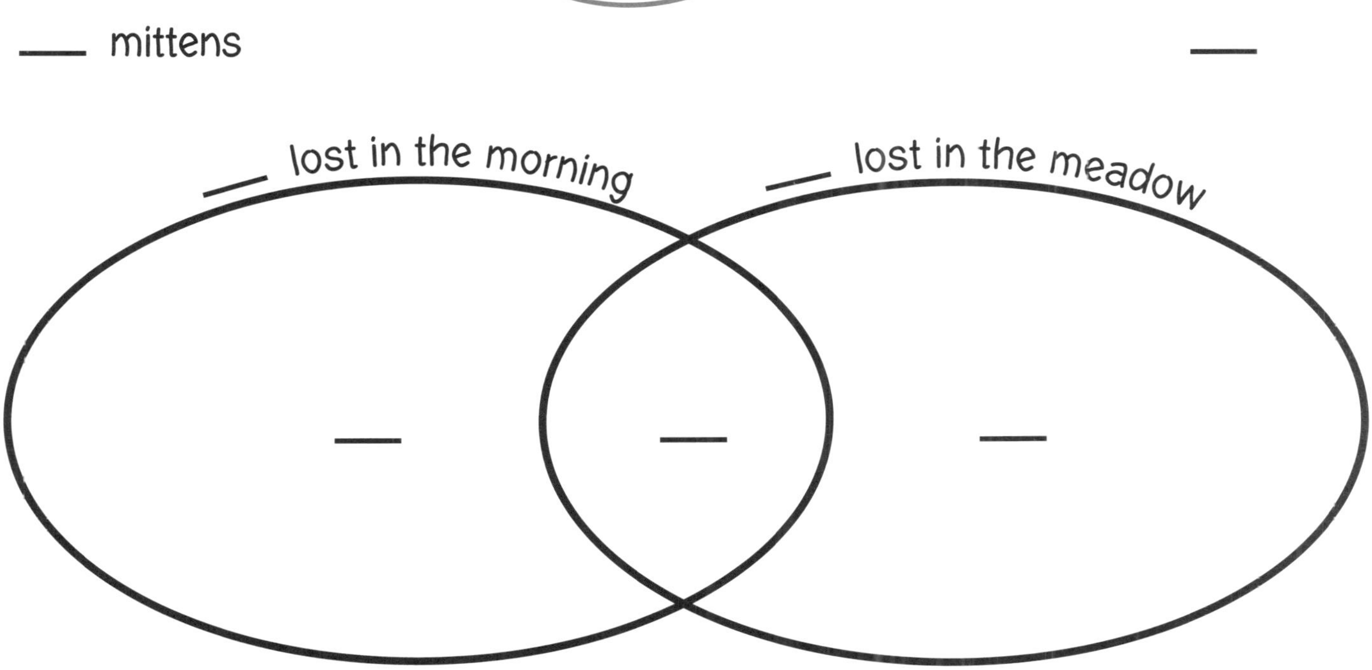

How many were not lost in the meadow in the morning? ______

Venn Perplexors

The Rhyme

A dillar, a dollar,
A ten-o'clock scholar,
What makes you come so soon?
You used to come at ten o'clock,
And now you come at noon.

The Clues

During the month of October (which started on a Monday and had no holidays) the 10 o'clock scholar arrived late to school 15 times.

He forgot his homework 18 times. Sadly, on 12 of those days, he forgot his homework and was late.

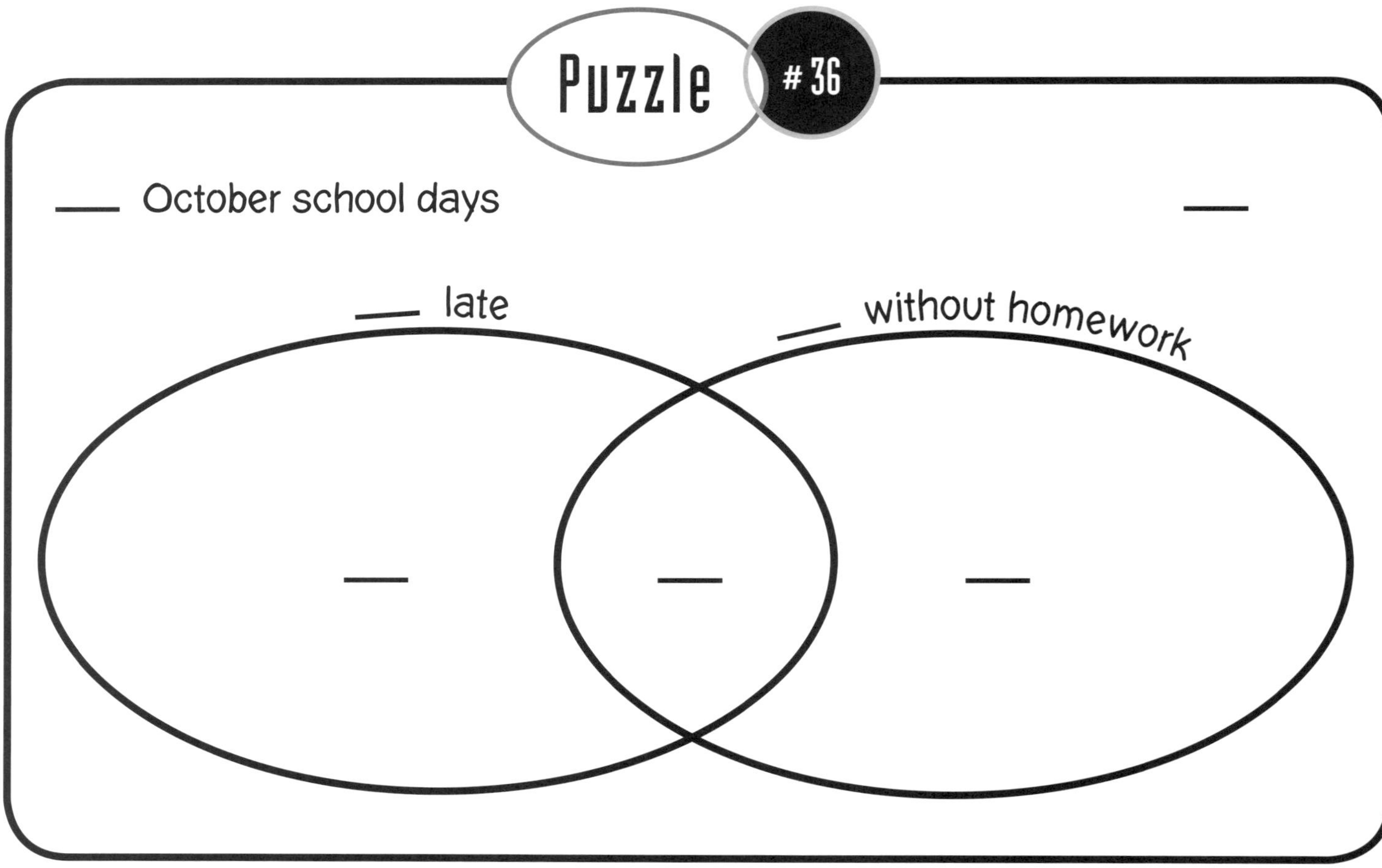

How many days in October did he arrive on time with his homework?

______

Venn Perplexors

The Rhyme

Old Mother Goose,
When she wanted to wander,
Would ride through the air
On a very fine gander.

Think of things that belong in each of the 4 areas of the diagram. Write 4 of them in each section.

Puzzle # 37

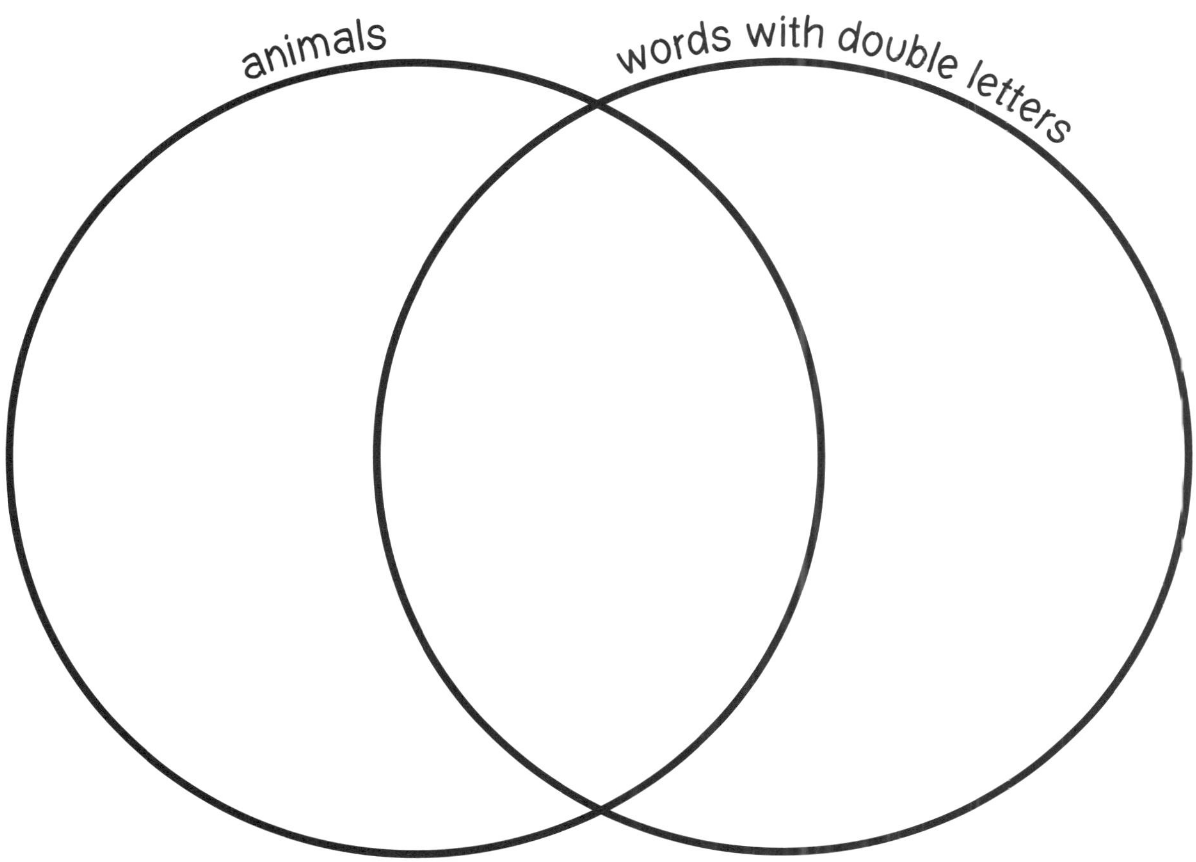

Venn Perplexors

The Rhyme

Great A, little a,
Bouncing B,
The cat's in the cupboard
And can't see me!

Think of things that belong in each of the 4 areas of the diagram. Write 4 of them in each section.

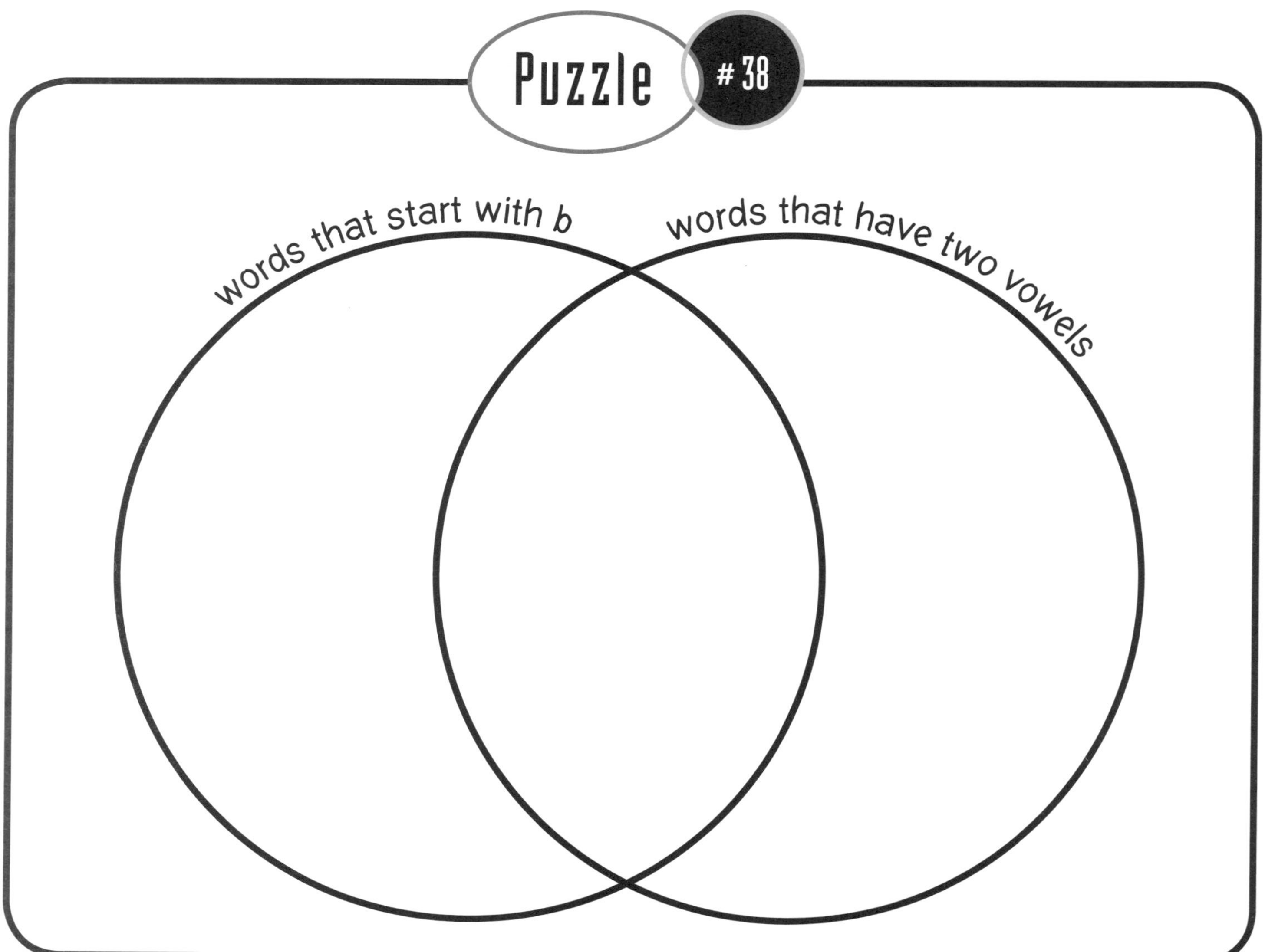

Venn Perplexors

The Rhyme

I bought a dozen new-laid eggs
Off good old Farmer Dickens;
I hobbled home upon two legs
And found them full of chickens!

Think of things that belong in each of the 4 areas of the diagram. Write 4 of them in each section.

Puzzle #39

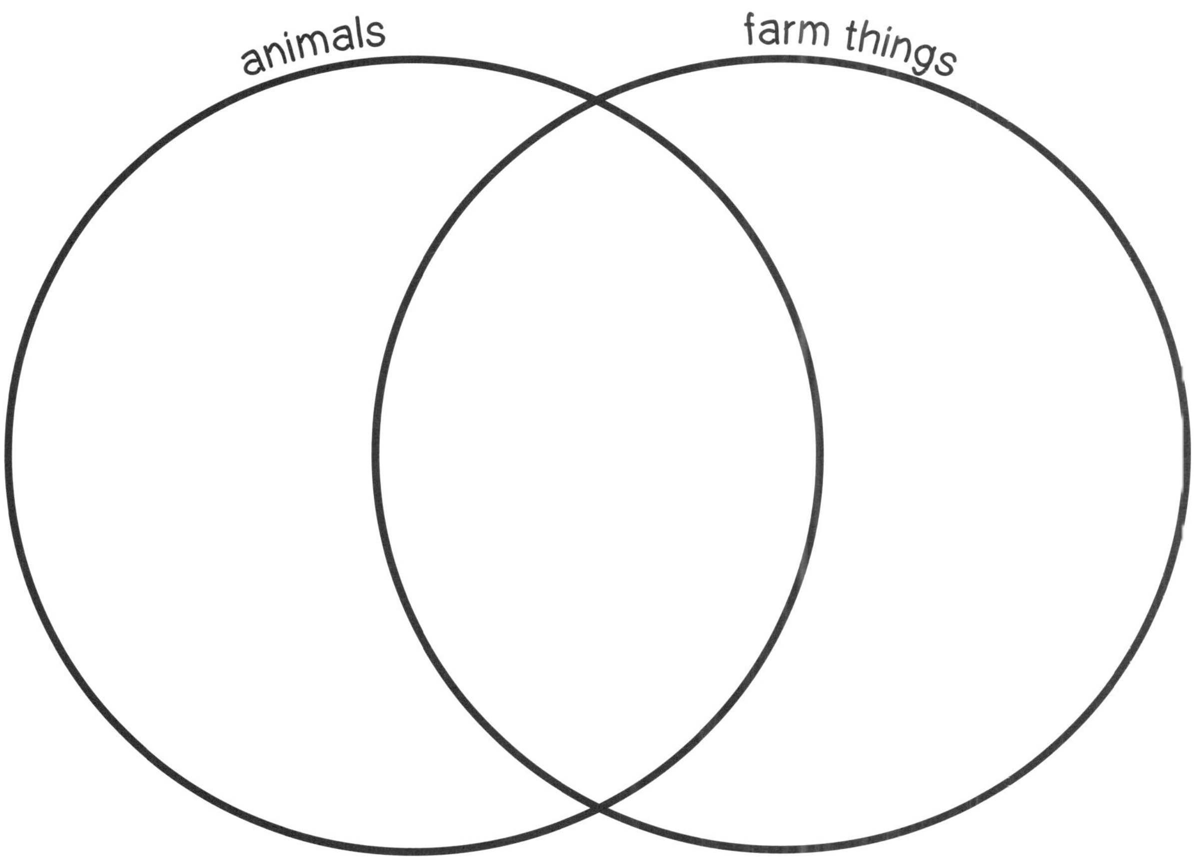

Venn Perplexors

The Rhyme

I had a little nut tree, nothing would it bear,
But a silver nutmeg and a golden pear.
The king of Spain's daughter came to visit me,
And all for the sake of my little nut tree.

Think of things that belong in each of the 4 areas of the diagram. Write 4 of them in each section.

Puzzle #40

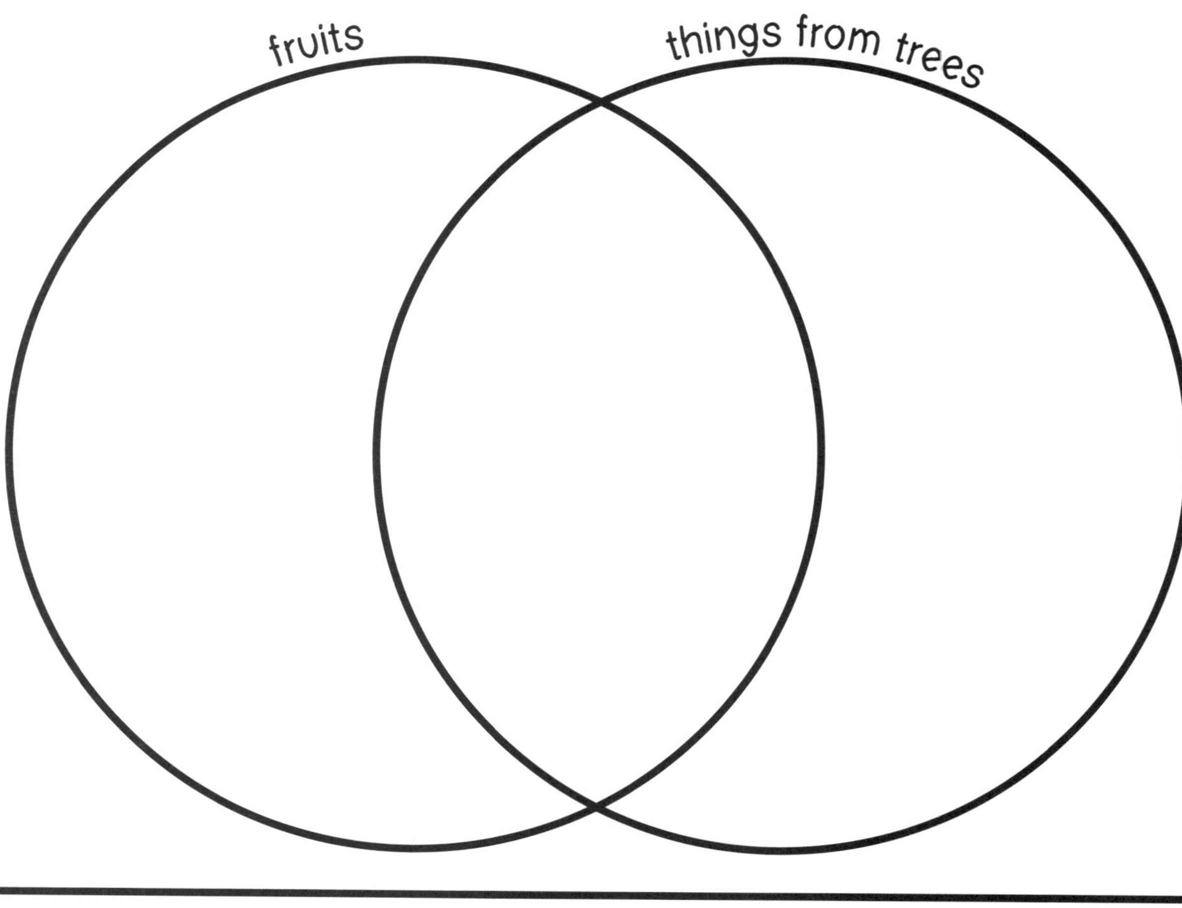

Venn Perplexors

The Rhyme

1, 2, 3, 4, 5,
I caught a hare alive!
6, 7, 8, 9, 10,
I let him go again!

Think of things that belong in each of the 4 areas of the diagram. Write 4 of them in each section.

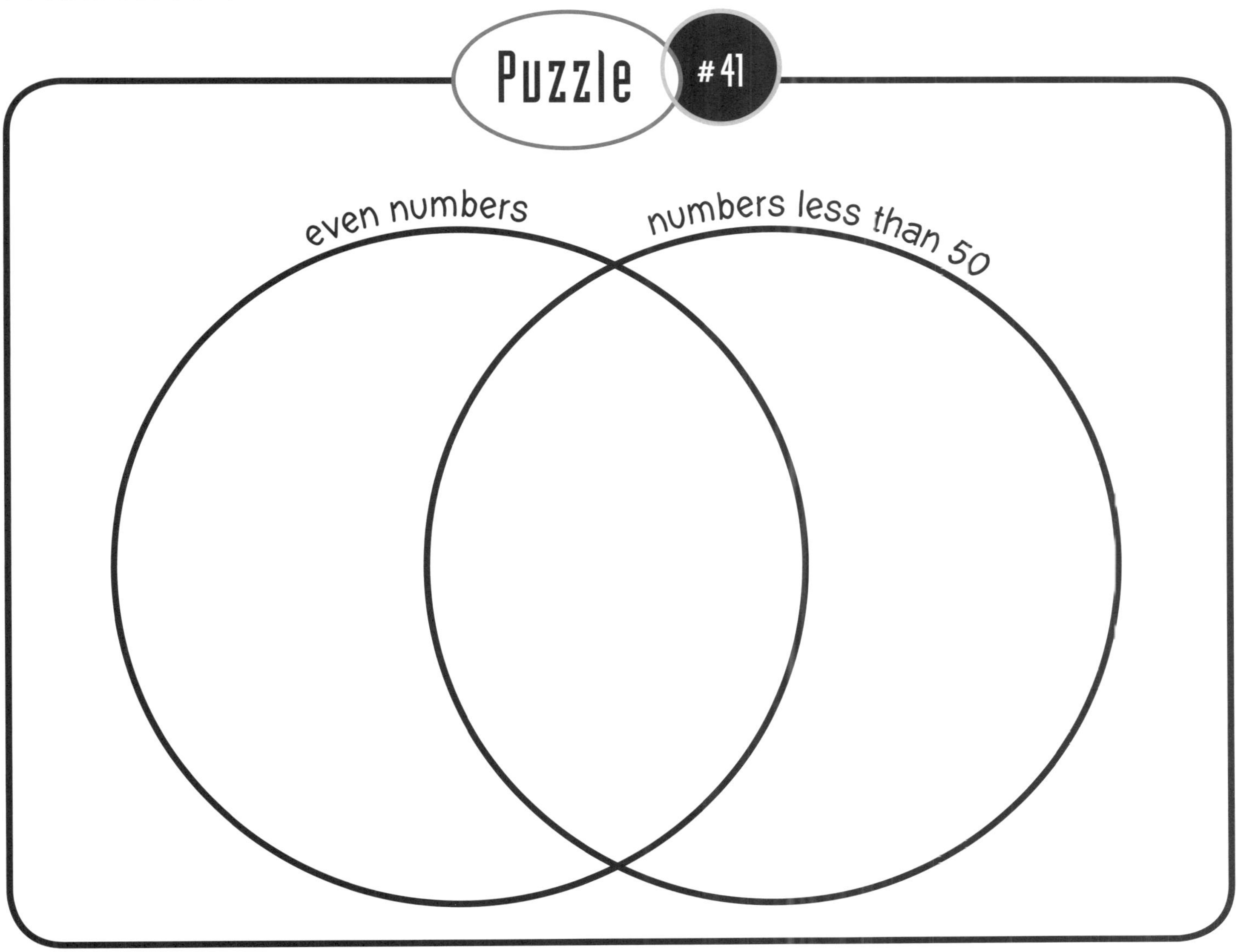

Venn Perplexors

The Rhyme

Donkey, donkey, old and gray,
Open your mouth and gently bray;
Lift your ears and blow your horn,
To wake the world this sleepy morn.

Think of things that belong in each of the 4 areas of the diagram. Write 4 of them in each section.

Puzzle #42

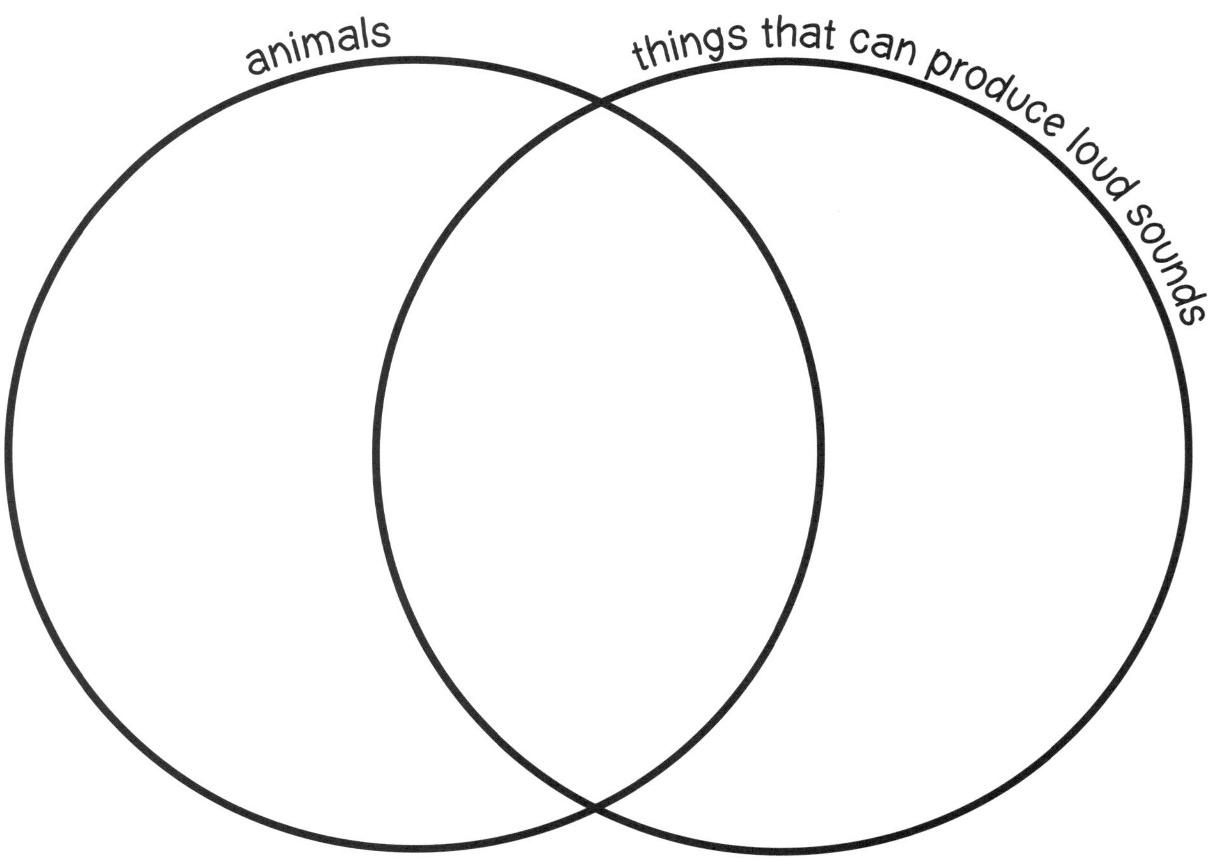

Venn Perplexors

The Rhyme

Humpty Dumpty sat on a wall,
Humpty Dumpty had a great fall;
All the king's horses and all the king's men,
Couldn't put Humpty together again.

Think of things that belong in each of the 4 areas of the diagram. Write 4 of them in each section.

Puzzle #43

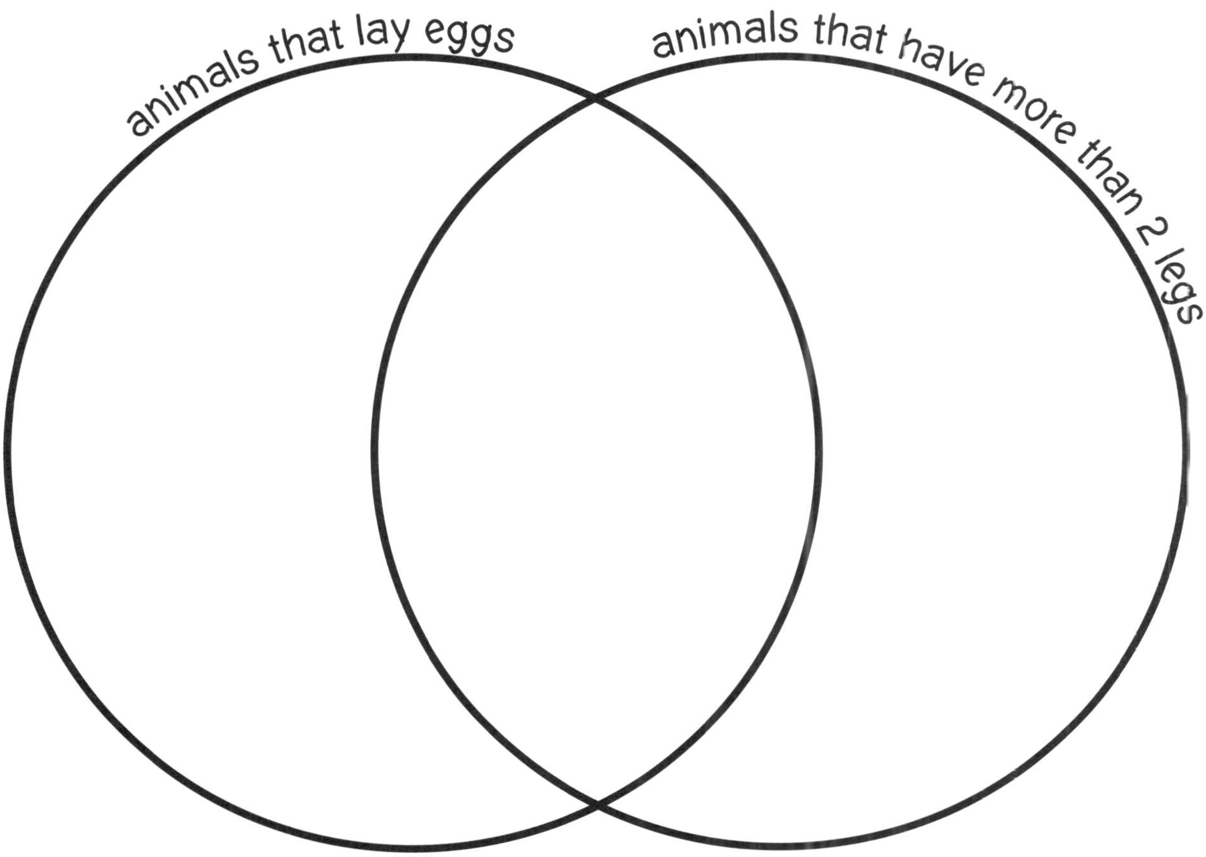

Venn Perplexors

The Rhyme

Jack be nimble,
Jack be quick,
Jack jump over
The candlestick.

Think of things that belong in each of the 4 areas of the diagram. Write 4 of them in each section.

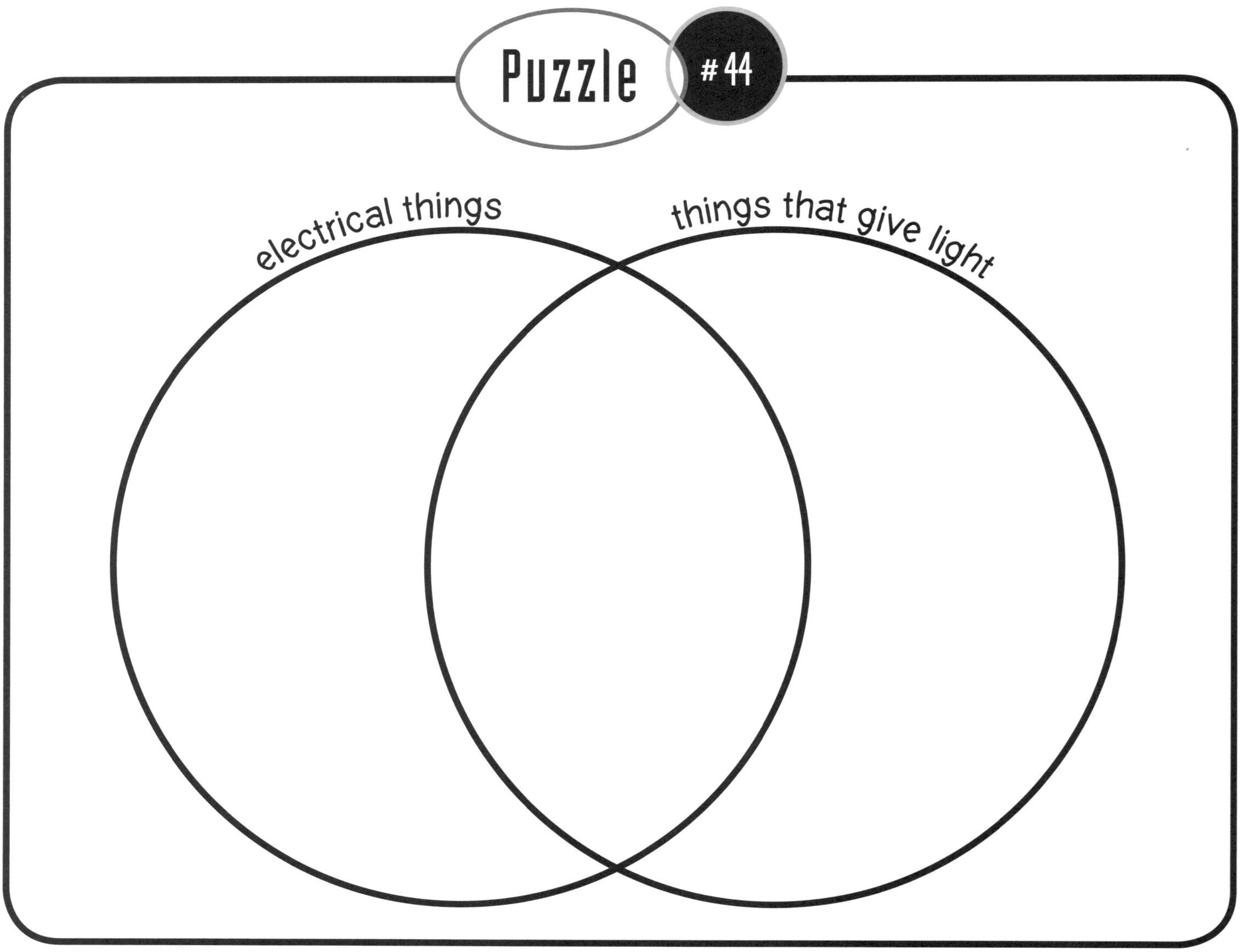

Venn Perplexors

The Rhyme

Tom, Tom, the piper's son,
Learned to play when he was young,
But the only tune that he could play
Was 'Over the hills and far away.'

Think of things that belong in each of the 4 areas of the diagram. Write 4 of them in each section.

Puzzle #45

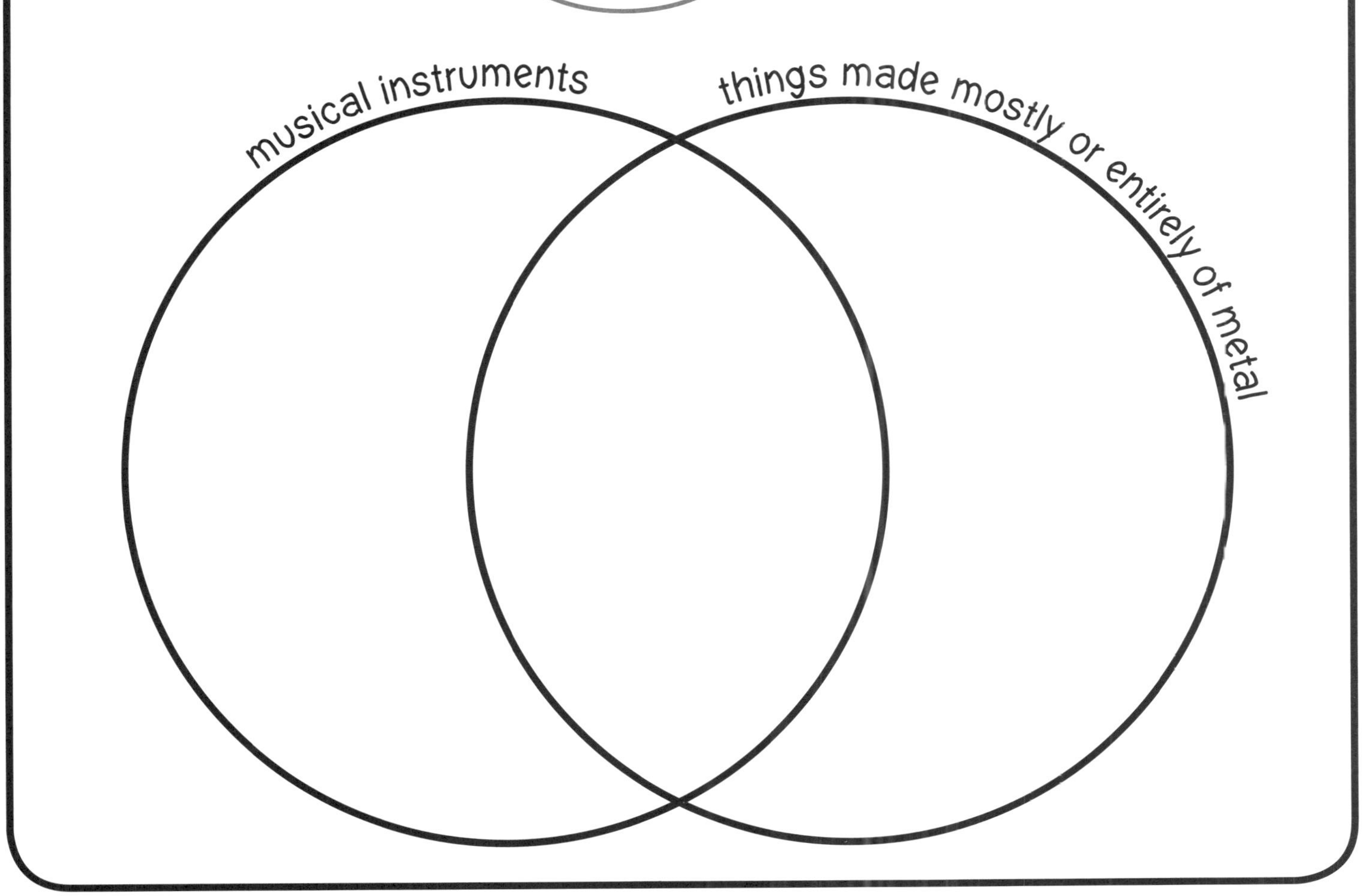

Venn Perplexors

The Rhyme

Cackle, cackle, Madam Goose!
Have you any feathers loose?
Truly, have I, little fellow,
Half enough to fill a pillow;
And here are quills, take one or two,
And down to make a bed for you.

Think of things that belong in each of the 4 areas of the diagram. Write 4 of them in each section.

Puzzle #46

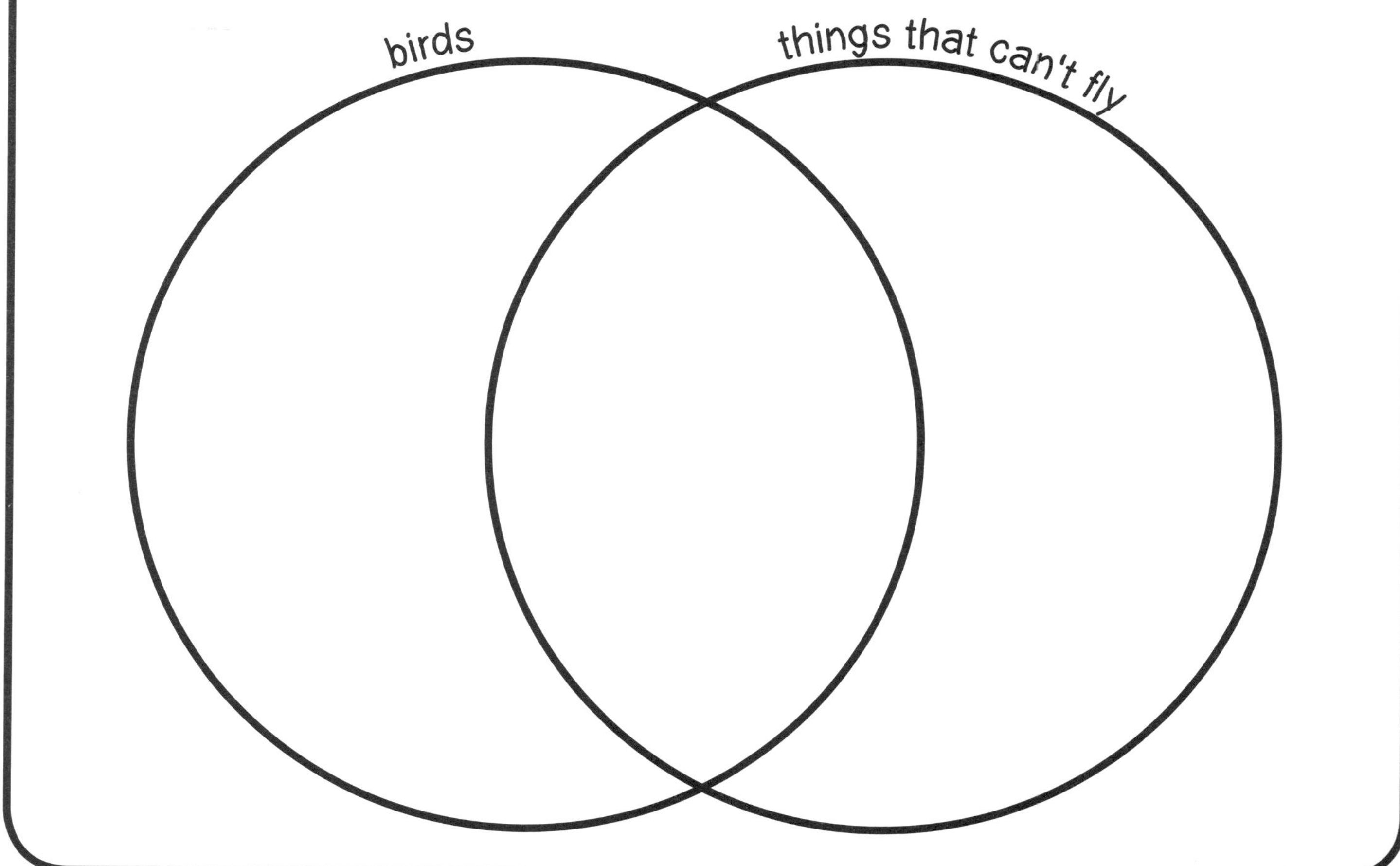

Venn Perplexors

The Rhyme

Twinkle, twinkle, little star,
How I wonder what you are!
Up above the world so high,
Like a diamond in the sky.
Twinkle, twinkle, little star,
How I wonder what you are!

Think of things that belong in each of the 4 areas of the diagram. Write 4 of them in each section.

Puzzle #47

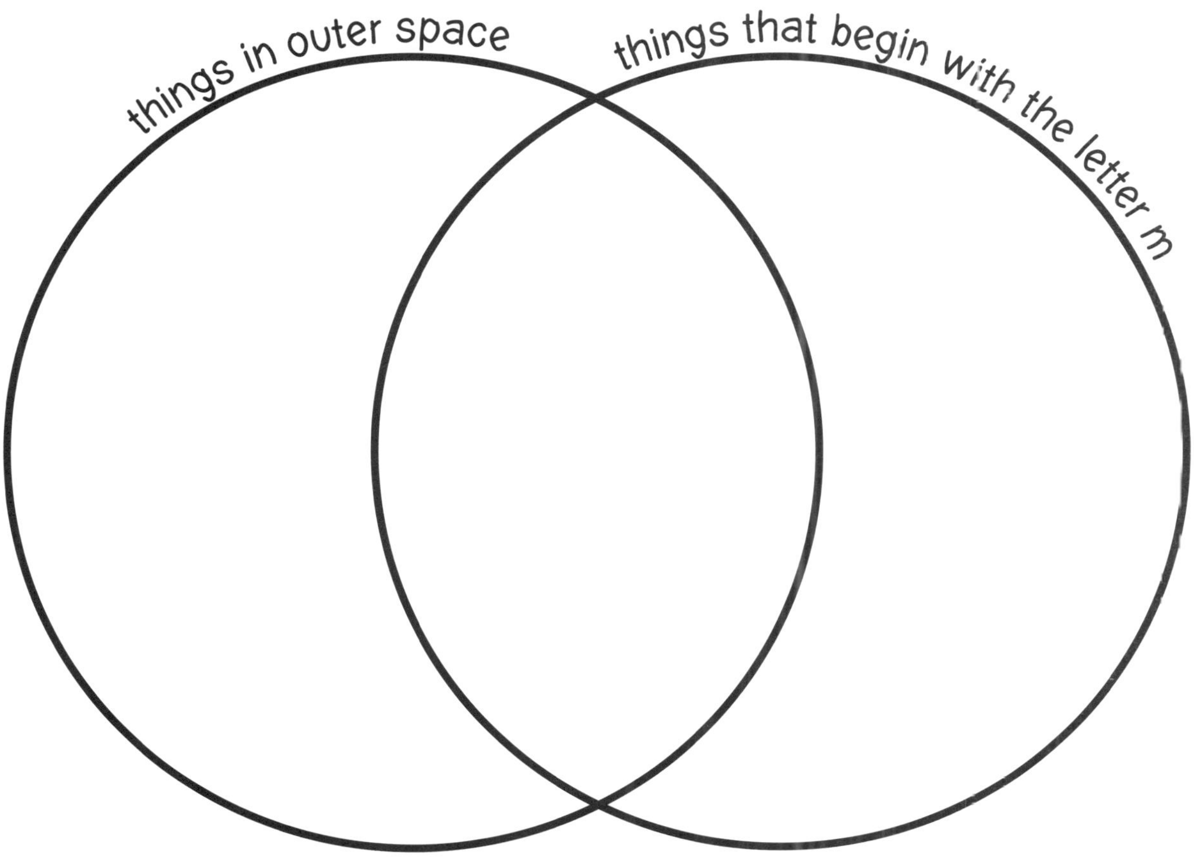

Venn Perplexors

The Rhyme

Row, row, row your boat,
Gently down the stream.
Merrily, merrily, merrily, merrily,
Life is but a dream.

Think of things that belong in each of the 4 areas of the diagram. Write 4 of them in each section.

Puzzle #48

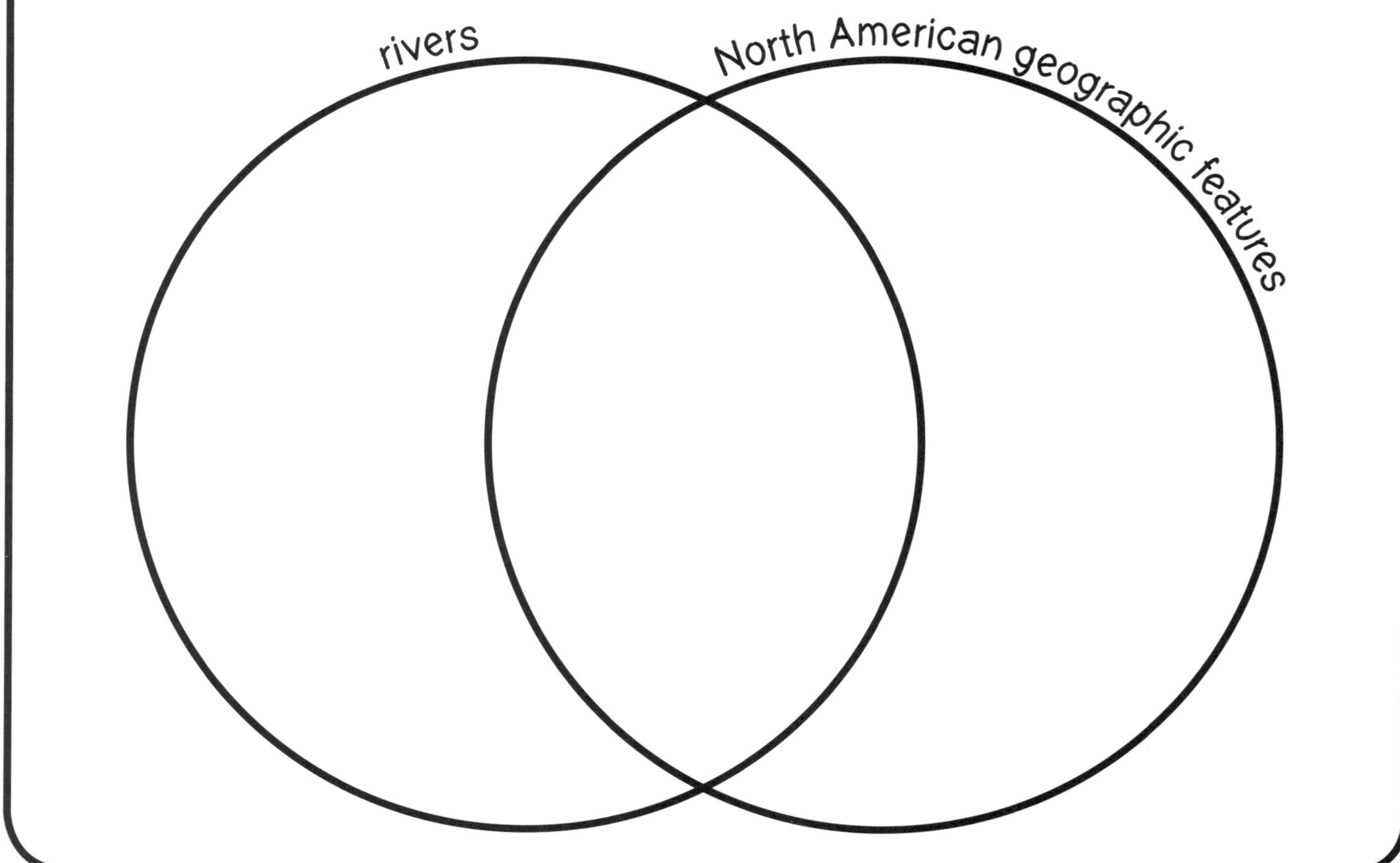

Venn Perplexors SOLUTIONS

#1

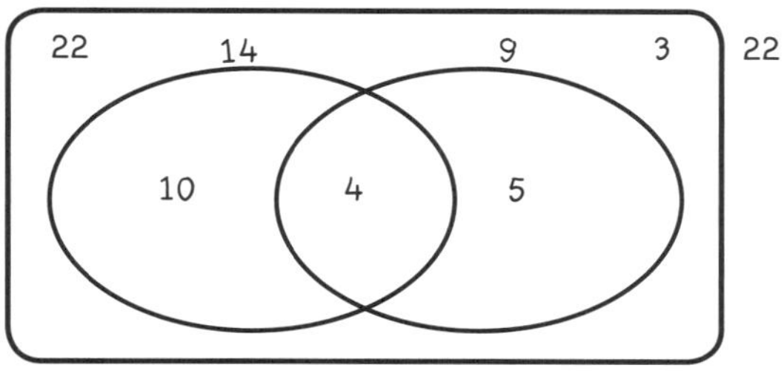

#2

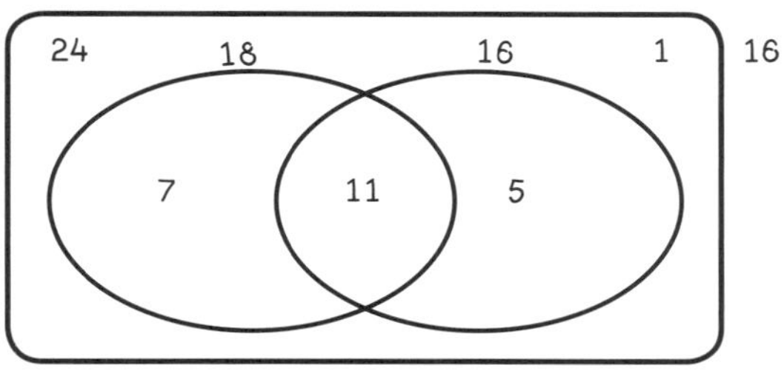

#3

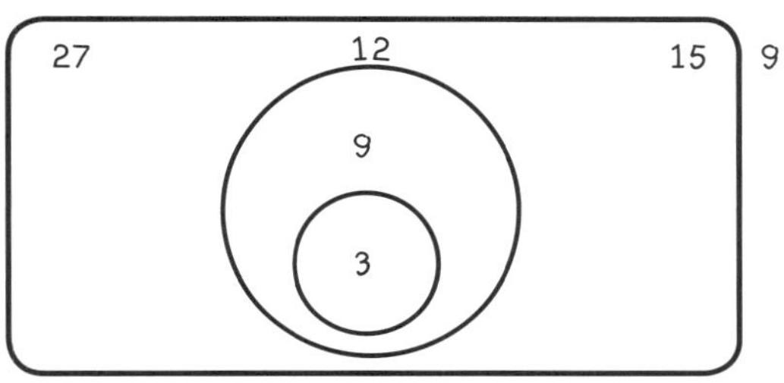

#4

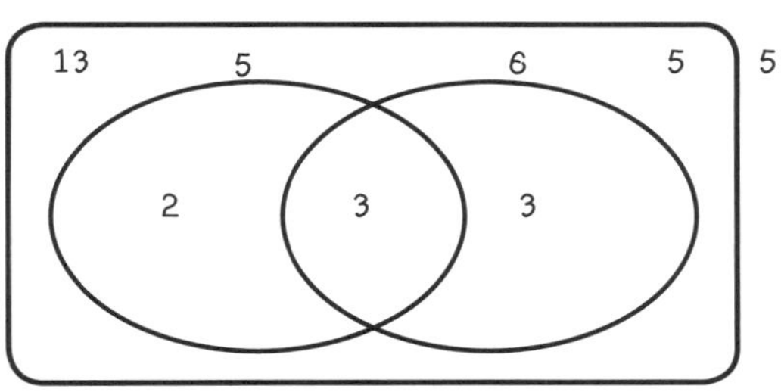

#5

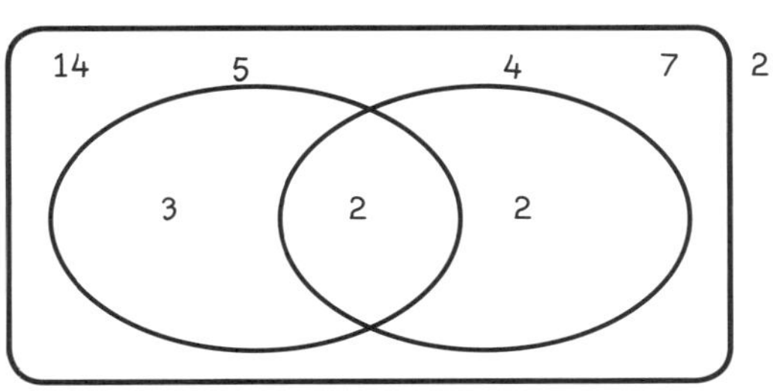

#6

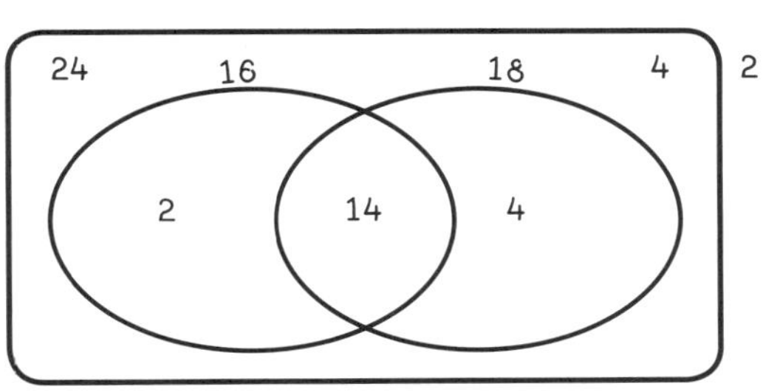

#7

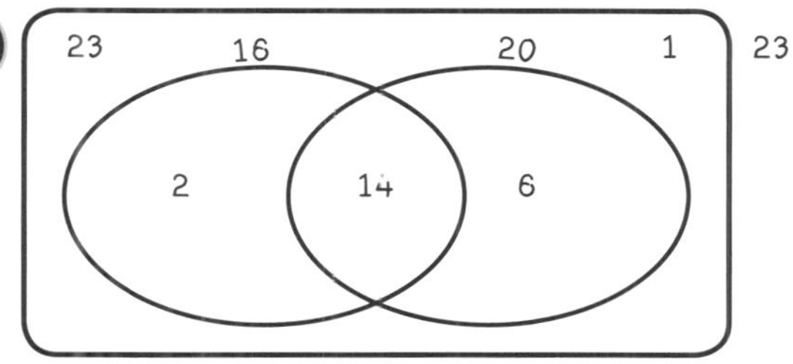

#8

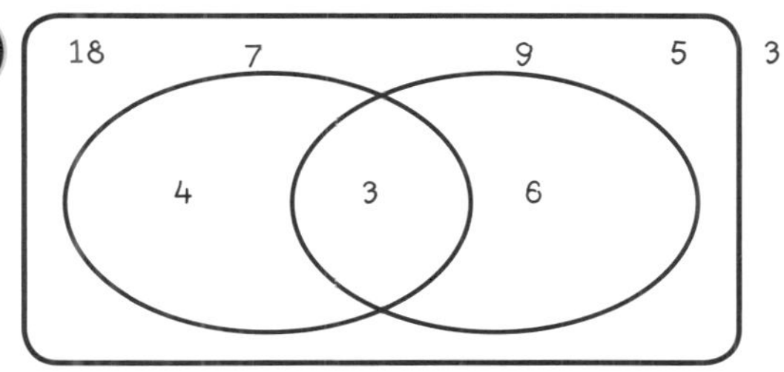

#9

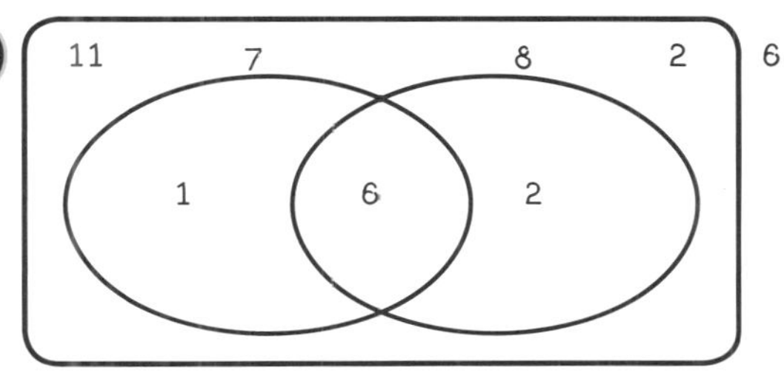

#10

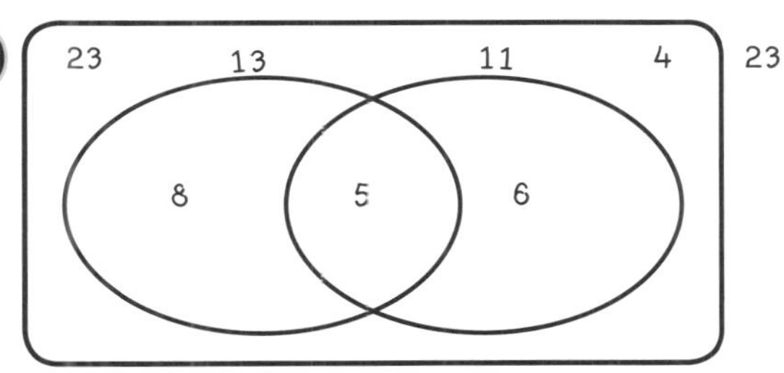

#11

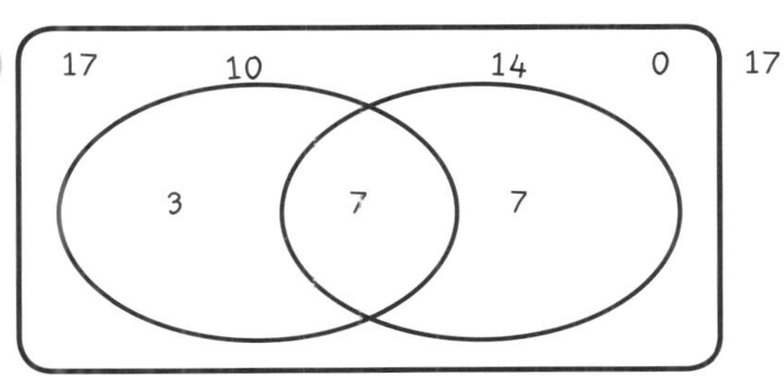

#12

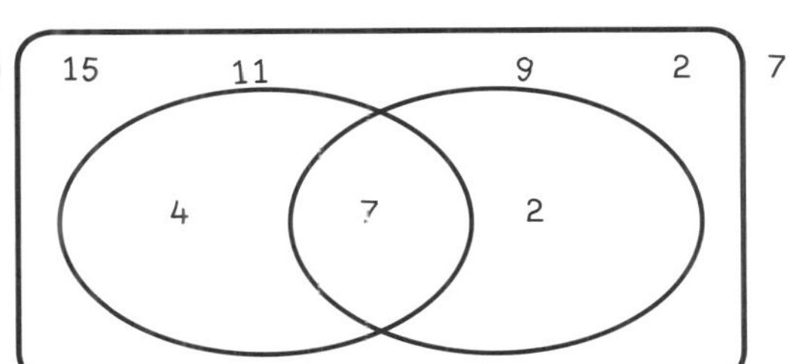

Venn Perplexors SOLUTIONS

#13
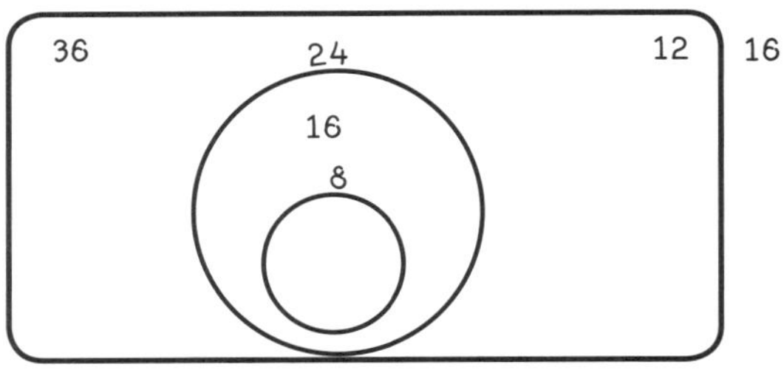

#14
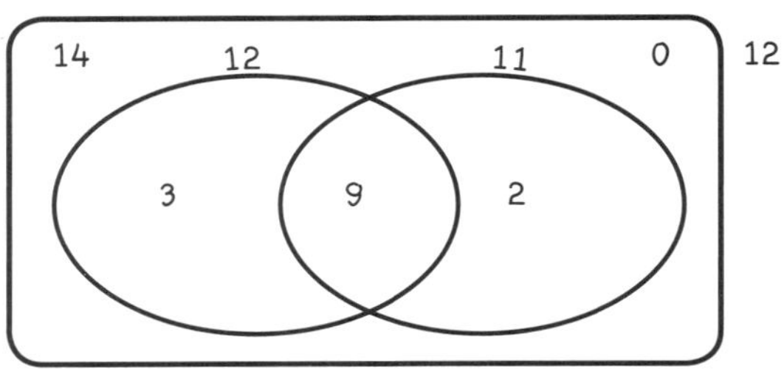

#15
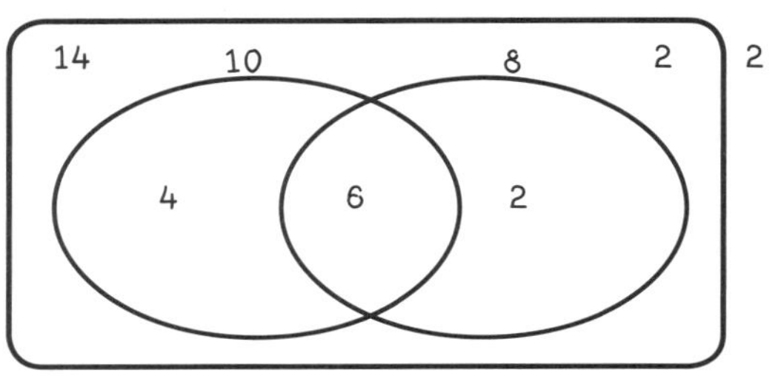

#16
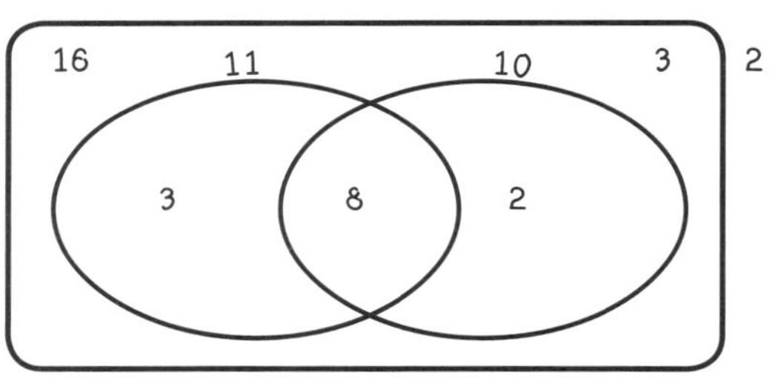

#17
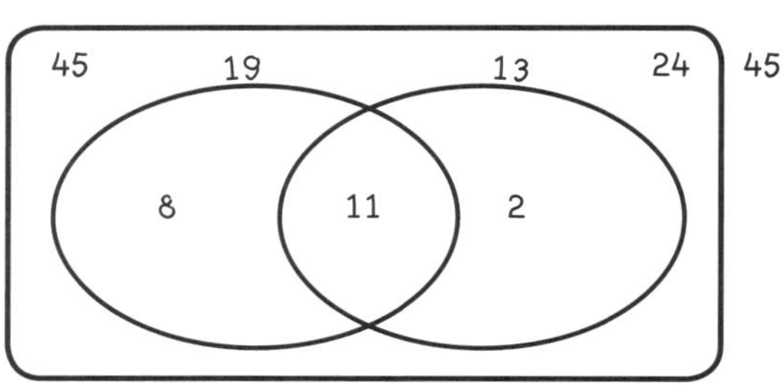

#18
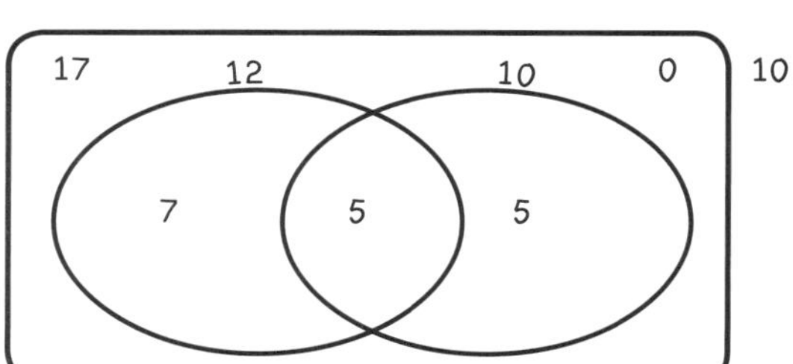

#19
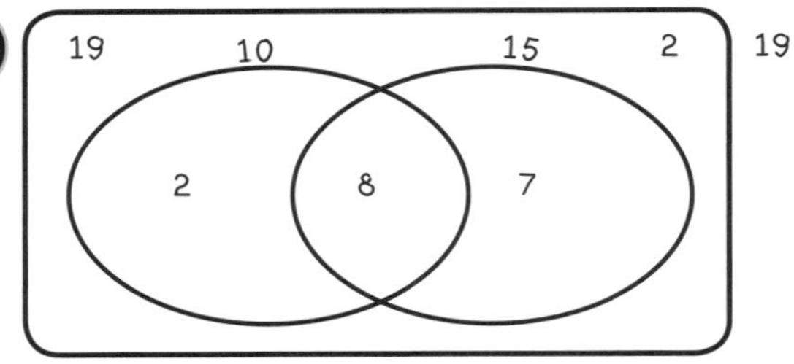

#20
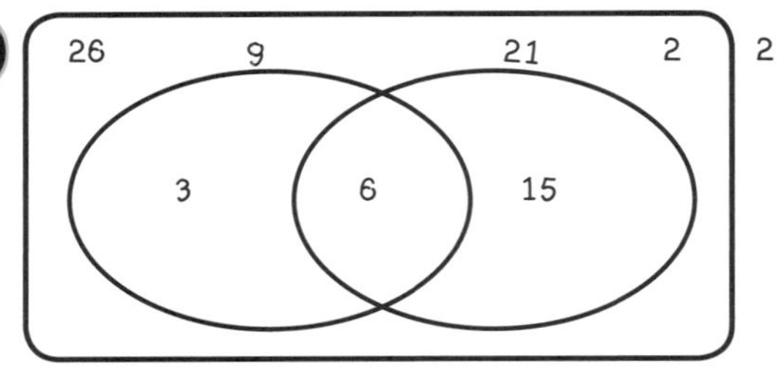

#21
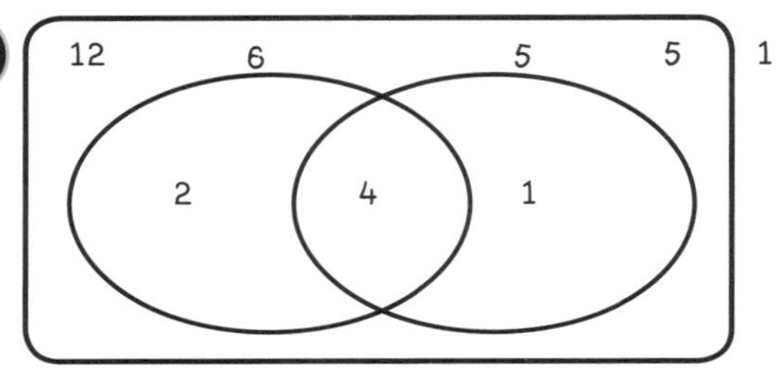

#22
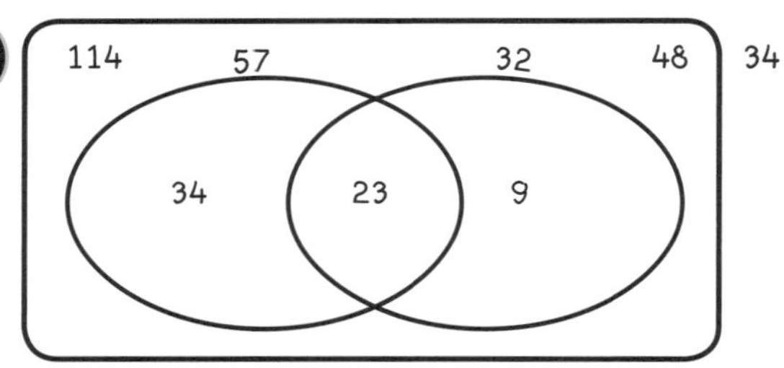

#23
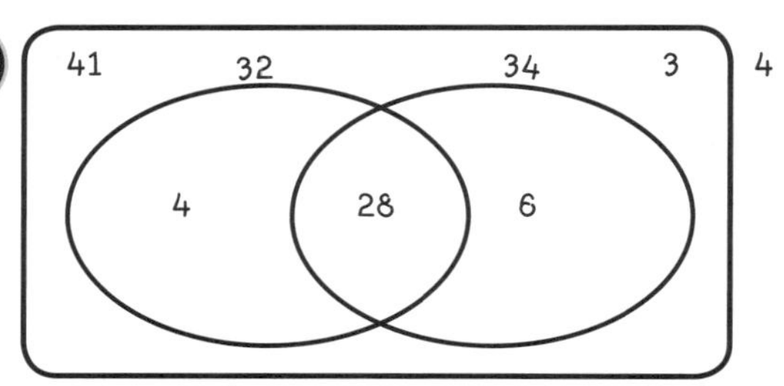

#24
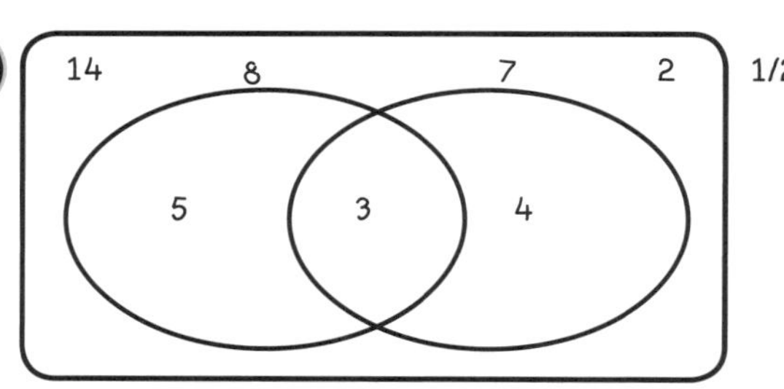

Venn Perplexors SOLUTIONS

#25
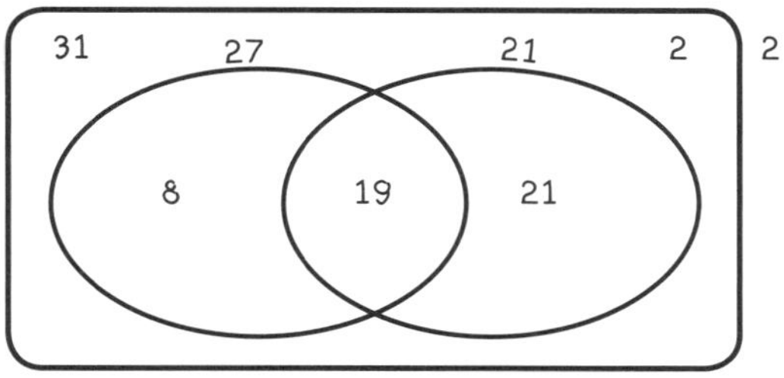

#26
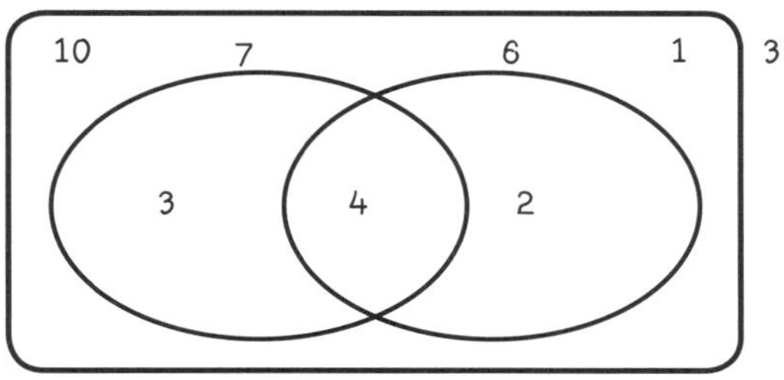

#27
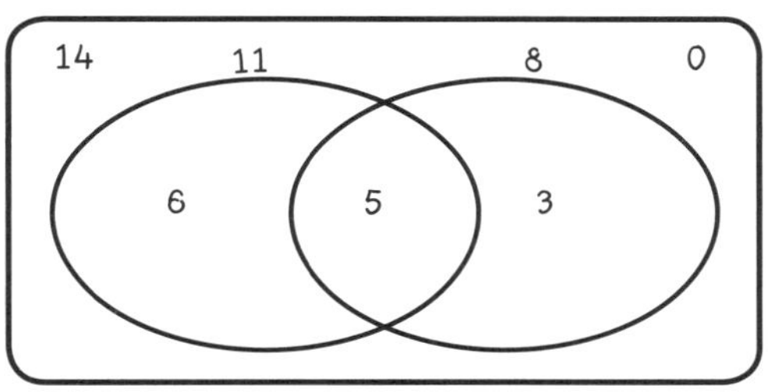

#28
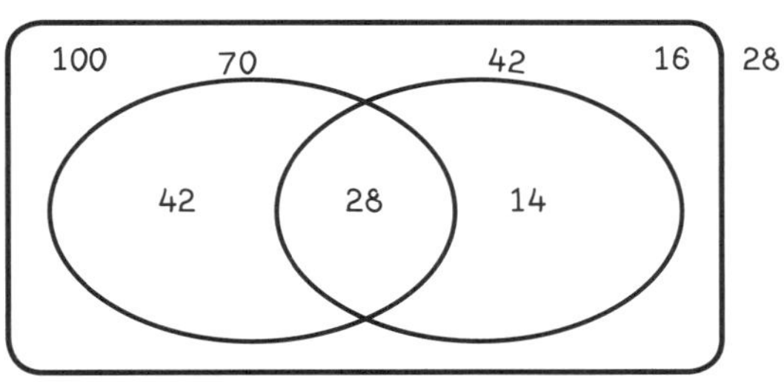

#29
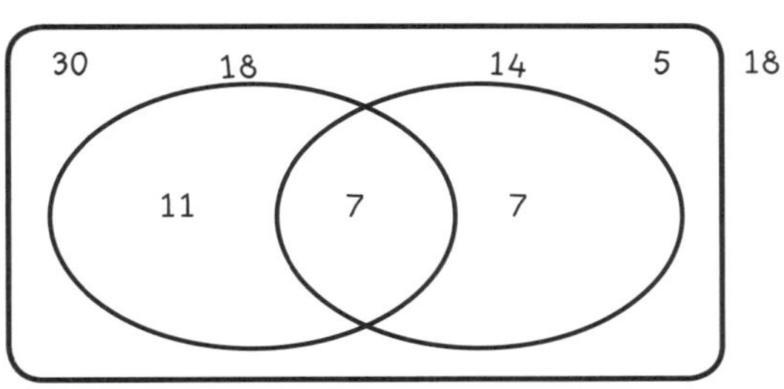

#30
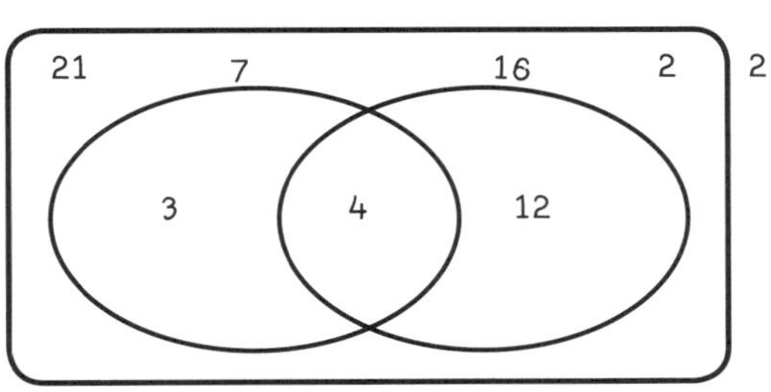

#31
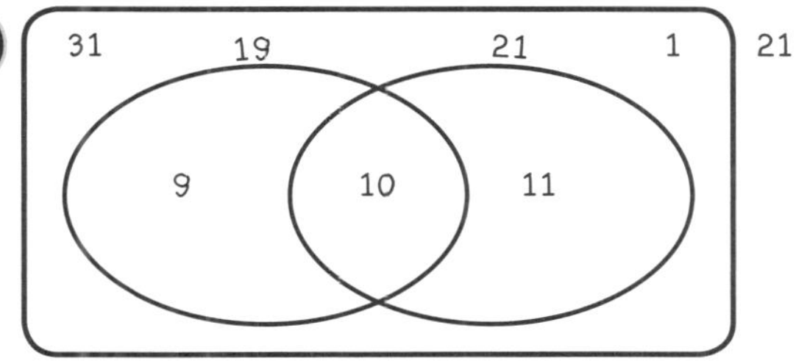

#32
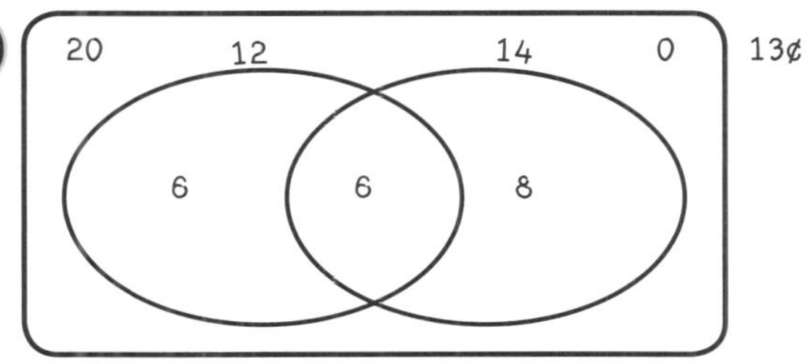

#33
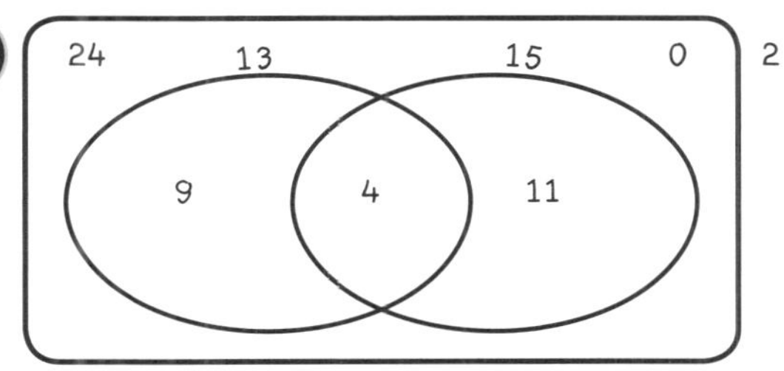

#34
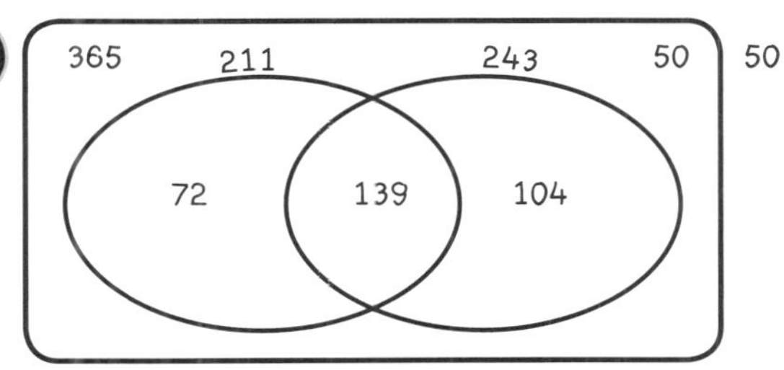

#35
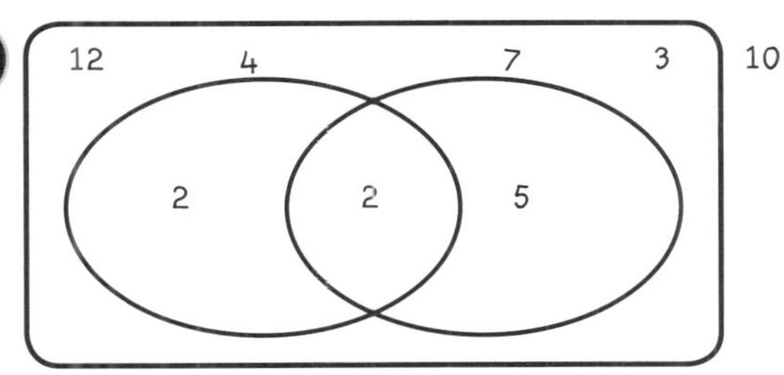

#36
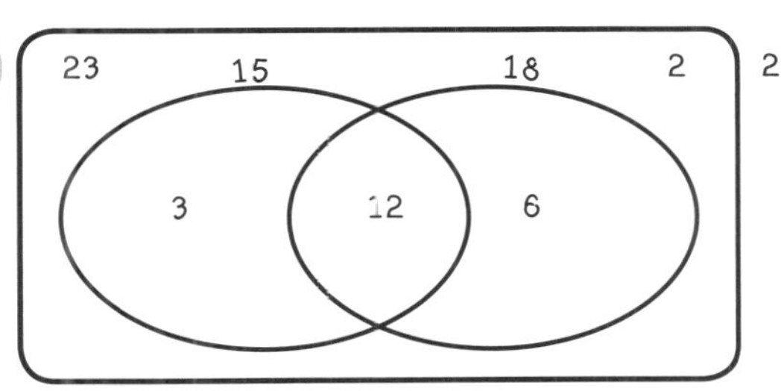

Venn Perplexors SOLUTIONS

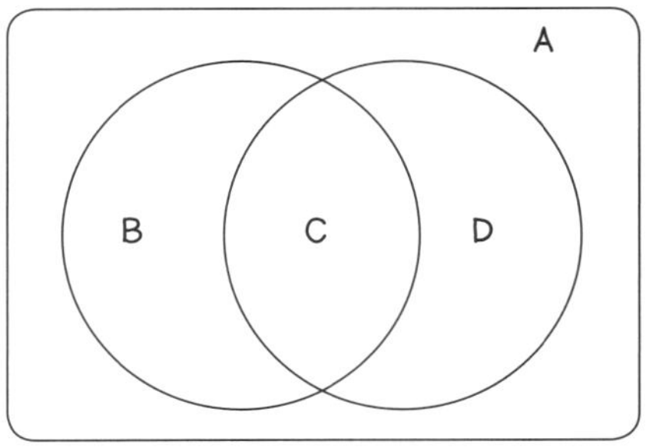

In the following puzzles the answers refer to the sections denoted by the letters below. These are sample answers only. Responses will vary.

#37
A: rock, kite, purple, flower
B: fox, eagle, lizard, frog
C: goose, kitten, rabbit, gull
D: cheese, egg, spoon, little

#38
A: cat, sum, talk, fun
B: bug, bat, best, black
C: bead, blue, bone, beef
D: read, pie, toe, four

#39
A: star, cactus, school, Mars
B: lion, giraffe, wolf, zebra
C: cow, sheep, horse, pig
D: tractor, barn, silo, plow

#40
A: grass, rose, rock, jet
B: grape, strawberry, pineapple, watermelon
C: pear, apple, lemon, kiwi
D: paper, wood, rubber, bark

#41
A. 71, 83, 145, 2469
B. 68, 92, 388, 1576
C: 10, 4, 36, 28
D: 3, 27, 49, 31

#42
A: feather, moon, thread, cotton ball
B: clam, butterfly, slug, barnacle
C: donkey, tiger, elephant, rooster
D: siren, trumpet, radio, tornado

#43
A: gorilla, human, seal, pizza
B: robin, tuna, snake, seahorse
C: platypus, frog, turtle, butterfly
D: camel, skunk, cheetah, goat

#44
A: brick, flag, baseball, daffodil
B: mixer, washer, dryer, can opener
C: flashlight, laser pointer, traffic light, computer
D: sun, firefly, match, candle

#45
A: hug, star, heart, banana
B: violin, recorder, bagpipe, zither
C: trumpet, trombone, cymbals, piccolo
D: penny, ring, pan, staples

#46
A: kite, helicopter, jet, rocket
B: wren, pelican, falcon, cardinal
C: penguin, ostrich, emu, rhea
D: cat, dog, elephant, rhinoceros

#47
A: pizza, oak, hamster, daisy
B: star, Jupiter, asteroid, comet
C: moon, Mars, Mercury, meteor
D: maple, mink, moss, me

#48
A: spaghetti, book, computer, cat
B: Nile, Amazon, Danube, Yangtze
C: Mississippi, Potomac, Colorado, Columbia
D: Great Salt Lake, Death Valley, Mammoth Cave, Rocky Mountains

